Although every attempt has been made to ensure that the information in this document is accurate and complete, some typographical errors or technical inaccuracies may exist. The Integration Consortium does not accept responsibility for any kind of loss resulting from the use of information contained in this document. The information contained in this document is subject to change without notice.

The incorporation of the product attributes discussed in these materials into any release or upgrade of any Informatica software product—as well as the timing of any such release or upgrade—is at the sole discretion of Informatica.

This edition published May 2005

Copyright © 2005 Informatica Corporation. All rights reserved. Printed in the U.S.A. Informatica, the Informatica logo, PowerCenter, and PowerChannel are trademarks or registered trademarks of Informatica Corporation in the United States and in jurisdictions throughout the world. All other company and product names mentioned herein may be tradenames or trademarks of their respective owners.

Acknowledgements

Integration as a discipline is an emerging field requiring a broad spectrum of capabilities. The insights contained in this book were collected over the course of 10 years from many IT practitioners, including systems architects, software engineers, industry analysts, executives, and academic researchers. From this perspective, the book itself is an act of integration.

However, a handful of individuals have impacted this book more than others and deserve special recognition for their thought leadership and for putting their ideas into practice. **Charlie Betz** is a leader in integration metadata disciplines and the concept of ERP for IT; he made several major contributions to this book. **Chris Capadouca** and **Greg Friesen** are from a rare breed of enterprise architects who can communicate effectively at a strategic and conceptual level yet roll up their sleeves and get their hands dirty at just about any level of detail anyone would care to tackle. **Howard Seidel** is about 10 years ahead of everyone else, but it's not just talk; he is constantly testing his theories in real-world practical scenarios.

Matthew Polly was the driving force behind this book and the sole person responsible for clearing all hurdles necessary to make this book happen. Without his tireless efforts and commitment to making the vision of an authoritative reference on integration competency centers become reality, this project would not have been possible. **John Herstein, Jarrod Buckley, Steven Fleishman,** and **Stephen Dulzer** are enterprise architects who can pinpoint problems and see solutions through the relentless fog of even the most complex IT systems. Their contribution was tremendous.

With grateful appreciation to you all—we couldn't have done it without you.

Contents

Foreword

In the 1900s, Ford Motor Company revolutionized the automobile industry with the assembly line—transforming the process of making custom automobiles to turning out Model Ts at the rate of almost two million a year. While the assembly line was the enabling technology for this remarkable feat, just as important to Ford's success were the processes, best practices and people behind the assembly line.

Some of the same approaches that Ford used to dominate the auto industry help today's companies to gain control over this increasingly complex IT challenge of enterprise integration. Just as the early years of auto manufacturing evolved from custom jobs to assembly lines, the problem of integration has evolved from one-off projects to the repeatable, sustainable structure of an Integration Competency Center.

An Integration Competency Center allows forward-looking organizations to apply the same attention to processes, best practices and people that Ford did to his assembly line—turning a jumble of ad-hoc integration projects into a coordinated, efficient and timely integration strategy.

In this groundbreaking book, Lyle and Schmidt highlight the significant benefits IT organizations can realize by adopting a more centralized integration approach, gaining efficiencies and cost savings that ultimately can translate into a corporate competitive differentiator. Describing the various "flavors" of an ICC that can be adopted by companies depending on their needs, Lyle and Schmidt then lay out a best-practices approach to implementing a centralized integration model—from assigning the right people, to determining processes and selecting the best technology.

Just as Ford changed the way businesses manufactured items through the use of technology, today's enterprises can dramatically improve the success and reduce the cost of their integration projects by combining integration technologies with best practices, standardization and the strategic resources of an ICC.

This is a must-read book for any IT organization seeking to maximize their IT investments for business advantage.

David Stodder
Editor-in-Chief, Intelligent Enterprise

Chapter 1

Seize the Integration Advantage

The integration competency center (ICC) is an enterprise shared service for performing systematic application integration. The goals of the ICC are to:

1. **Reduce integration costs** so that a larger percentage of the IT budget can be focused on business value-added systems. The ICC does this by enforcing standards, using highly tuned processes, and driving software and data reuse. The result is less development effort, reduced need for extensive testing, and lower support costs.

2. **Create an adaptive enterprise** and allow the business to rapidly change as the market changes. The ICC does this by allowing individual applications to be loosely coupled so that they can change independently yet still be tightly integrated to enable efficient business processes.

The ICC can be deployed in one of five models, depending on organizational structure, maturity of business processes, enterprise architecture discipline, geographic distribution of IT functions, and autonomy of business units. Each model provides business benefits, with the higher-maturity models adding the greatest value.

A growing number of references, including the preceding quotes, reinforce the trend toward establishing ICCs. However, few practical materials are available to help organizations get started. The purpose of this book is to correct that deficiency.

Implementing an ICC is not without risks. According to Gartner, in a November 2004 Research Note:

> *The top-performing one-third of ICCs will save an average of 30 percent in data interface development time and costs and 20 percent in maintenance costs, and achieve 25 percent reuse of integration component during 2004 through 2007 (.8 probability). The remaining two-thirds of ICCs will fall short of those benefits because of insufficient sponsorship and other organizational execution problem during 2004 through 2007 (.7 probability).*

Gartner, Inc., *Predicts 2005: Application Integration ESBs and B2B Evolve,* November 2004

In pre-ICC days, organizations lacked the ability to coordinate their integration efforts with all of the key parties, resulting in many failed or overly expensive integration efforts. ICCs are the missing ingredient that can provide this coordination ability.

Integration Competency Center Best Practices, Forrester Research, Inc. February 2005

Most large enterprises have what we call the *integration hairball.* An example appears in Figure 1, depicting major applications in an enterprise and their data dependencies. The hairball is characterized by unnecessary complexity resulting from duplicate systems, swivel chair integration (such as the unfortunate call center rep in the figure who must interact with 15 systems), high cost to deploy new systems, and unstable operations caused by changes with unknown dependencies.

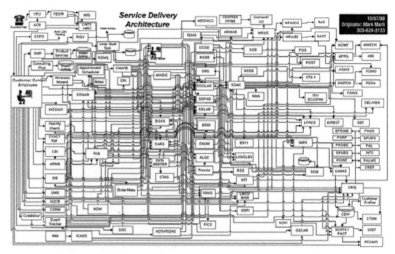

Figure 1-1. The Integration Hairball in Real Life

ICCs enable companies to integrate data and resources in a coherent, scalable, and cost-effective way to deliver an enduring competitive advantage. When done well, integration benefits the whole company. To ensure that your organization is among the top-performing one-third, read this book and visit the Integration Consortium Website at www.integrationconsortium.com for additional resources.

Chapter 2

Why Are ICCs Needed?

2.1 Integration Is a Distinct Discipline

The Integration Consortium defines integration as:

> *The process of integrating multiple applications that were separately developed, may use incompatible technology, and remain independently managed.*

For starters, integration is a process. More important, it is not a one-time process, but rather an ongoing activity, because the applications that are being integrated continue to change over time.

This independence is necessarily driven by "a separation of concerns," which is in turn a reaction to IT complexity. As complexity increases, it becomes necessary to break the problem into smaller, more manageable pieces; we call each manageable unit a *system*.

Applications (or simply systems) may themselves consist of other smaller systems, which are referred to as *subsystems*. An enterprise therefore has a hierarchy of systems; the collection of systems at the highest level is known as the *enterprise application portfolio*. The applications in the enterprise portfolio need to interoperate with each other and with the systems of external customers or suppliers. This highest level of integration within an enterprise is the scope of the integration competency center — the topic of this guidebook.

It is important to reinforce the point that a "system" is a logical concept, which means that it is subject to interpretation; in other words, a system is whatever you think it is. The implication of this statement is significant and helps to explain why developing the enterprise application portfolio is more of an agreement process than an analytical process. That said, it is useful to define a system as having one business owner, one IT owner, and one architect responsible for it.

A further implication is that a change in organizational structure may change the application portfolio. For example, if a business unit splits into two separate functions, what was previously considered one functional system supporting the unit may now need to be considered two separate functional systems.

See Chapter 8, section 8.6, for a detailed analysis of issues and standards related to system identification.

The collection of interfaces and middleware components that support the data movement and process interactions between systems in the application portfolio are called *integration systems*. Technically speaking, integration systems are similar to business systems: They are a collection of hardware components, software components, and data to support specific processes. The difference is that integration systems generally serve IT functions and cross-functional business needs rather than specific business units. From a technical perspective, five broad integration patterns can be delineated:

1. Data-oriented integration for consolidating and aggregating business intelligence

2. Message- (or file-)oriented integration for copying data to one or many systems

3. Process-oriented integration for managing long-running cross-functional business processes

4. Service oriented integration for handling real-time request/reply transactions between systems

5. Portal-oriented integration for providing a common end-user access to multiple systems

Each of these patterns may involve special protocols, standards, and technology. The computer industry's "holy grail" is to achieve a unified architecture for all five patterns, but as with Albert Einstein's lifelong search for a unified field theory that combined nuclear, electromagnetic, and gravitational forces, a unified integration architecture is not likely to emerge in our lifetime.

It is possible, however, for an ICC to establish the equivalent of a unified integration architecture within a given enterprise. When done well, this architecture will result in more efficient operations and rapid implementation of changes.

2.2 The Problem with Traditional Integration

To a person with a hammer, everything looks like a nail. Experience has shown that, regardless of requirements:

- People familiar with FTP will use it for all their integration requirements
- People familiar with file shares will use them
- People familiar with extract, transform, and load (ETL) will use it
- People familiar with databases will use them
- People familiar with queues will use them
- People familiar with application servers will use them

The result, in many large corporations, is an integration hairball.

The hairball is the result of years of incrementally building interfaces between applications by project teams operating in silos. In the absence of a prescriptive architecture, each team selects the tools with which they are most familiar and defines their own operational standards. In the absence of solid metadata and configuration management discipline, the team disbands at the end of the project, leaving behind documentation that is difficult to maintain—resulting in evaporation of tacit knowledge. Over time, the inconsistencies between interfaces and imperfect under- standing of dependencies between applications result in unstable opera- tions, production "surprises," high cost to maintain systems, and delays in implementing new business solutions.

The large number of interfaces in a Fortune 1000 company is not the issue. All modern enterprises have a diverse application portfolio that is necessary to compete in the marketplace and support the business. The issue is the inconsistency of integration standards and the lack of holistic understanding of dependencies, which creates unpredictability anytime there is a change. Scientists call this chaos. In other words, having a lot of hair is not the problem, but it is a problem if it's tangled and knotted into a hairball.

Here are some of the major challenges that organizations face in establishing consistent integration architectures:

- Inability to quantify and justify the investment in infrastructure initiatives
- Poor communication between the business units and the technology teams
- Business and IT alignment issues related to their respective priorities
- Ineffective change leadership

Although an ICC alone will not solve all of these challenges, it can play a pivotal role by bringing an enterprisewide focus to the issues. The role of leadership will be discussed in Chapter 5, but first let's take a closer look at the underlying drivers of these challenges: the integration laws.

2.3 Don't Break the Integration Laws

Integration "laws" are a way of thinking about the fundamental drivers of integration. The laws reflect the reality of dealing with "systems of systems" (or complex systems) that are characteristic of enterprise integration. They represent the reality of "what is" rather than "what could be" and, as with the laws of physics, describe many characteristics of the real world.

An effective integration approach must not conflict with the integration laws. Although challenging them won't land you in jail, ignoring them will likely add to the list of failed integration projects. As you start down the path of your ICC implementation, remember the following five laws.

2.3.1 Law 1: The Whole Is Greater Than the Sum of Its Parts

The notion of "process decomposition" is deeply ingrained in most analysis techniques used in software development life-cycle methodologies today. It is based on the presumption that there are natural boundaries along which to divide a complex system into smaller components for integration. This approach comes from the reductionist perspective, dealing with one dimension of problem analysis.

Although this approach helps tackle relatively simple problems in short time frames, it fails as system complexity increases and natural boundaries disappear. All of the gains achieved by breaking down the big problem are lost as the cost of integrating the small solutions becomes unworkable.

Most methodologies fail to realize that the essence of an end-to-end system cannot be captured by studying its individual components alone, and they fail to assign responsibility for the holistic solution. Or if accountability is clear for the initial construction of a solution, the solution can deteriorate if no one is responsible for sustaining the end-to-end processes on an ongoing basis.

2.3.2 Law 2: There Is No End State

Organizational entities split, merge, and morph into new structures. Political motivations and boundaries change. Technology evolves, and today's leading edge is tomorrow's legacy. An effective ICC approach must consider the full life cycle of a system and be based on best practices that recognize the adaptive nature of complex systems. From the start, we must plan for constant change.

Furthermore, ICCs must deal with legacy systems based on prior generations of technology. Many waves of application technology over the years seem to move in regular seven-year cycles (for example, mainframe to mini to microcomputers, monolithic to client/server to Web-service applications). The shift from one wave to the next is neither instantaneous nor is it necessarily economically valid to replace it. In fact, a given technology will usually last through several waves before it is fully replaced. Therefore, the ICC must deal with three or four generations of technology simultaneously.

2.3.3 Law 3: There Are No Universal Standards

Too many software standards have the same effect as no standards at all. Even successful standards (such as TCP/IP for the Internet) are not universal. When it comes to software standards such as COBOL or Java, interoperability and transportability come at the expense of vendor-specific extensions, forcing developers to use a less-than-ideal core set of "pure" language features.

The ICC should strive to define and adopt standards within the enterprise, but also work externally with standards organizations to gain agreement across the industry. In addition, the ICC must deal with the reality that many forces—including competition, the "not invented here" syndrome, and evolving technologies—will result in many different standards for the foreseeable future.

2.3.4 Law 4: Information Adapts to Meet Local Needs

The information engineering movement of the early 1990s was based on the incorrect notion that an enterprise can have a single consistent data model without redundancy. A more accurate way to look at information is this equation:

$$information = data + context$$

This formula says that the same data across different domains may have different meanings. For example, a simple attribute such as "current customer" can mean something different to the marketing, customer service, and legal departments. An extreme example is gender, which you might think could have only two states: male or female. One particular enterprise has defined 8 different genders. The same thing happens with natural languages (the various meanings and connotations that words receive in different communities). The ICC must embrace informational diversity, recognizing that variations exist, and use techniques to compensate for them.

2.3.5 Law 5: All Details Are Relevant

Abstraction is the practice of representing a problem without all the details, developing a model solution based on the abstract problem and then using the model to create the real-life solution. The success of this approach depends on our ability to build and use abstract models to manage and direct activities. But the effectiveness of an abstract model is inversely proportional to the complexity of the context, because no details can be safely ignored. The cost of developing and maintaining abstract models of the system and the project can become an economic black hole, consuming all benefits.

A successful ICC deals with this conundrum by decomposing the problem, yet maintaining a view of the entire picture. Although there is no easy solution, an effective ICC must strive to achieve dynamic models: those connected to the real world in such a way that when one changes, so does the other. Only then can we attain a truly sustainable integration infrastructure.

2.4 Integration Is a Competitive Differentiator

Your competitors can buy the same software from enterprise resource planning (ERP) vendors and industry solution providers, so how can you differentiate your company from others using information technology? The answer lies not in optimizing the parts, but in optimizing the whole through effective end-to-end integration of business processes and information.

Nicholas Carr, in his now-famous article, "IT Doesn't Matter," in the May 2003 issue of *Harvard Business Review*, made the point that information technology is a commodity. In one respect he was right. Individual IT components, such as PCs, servers, disk farms, and off-the-shelf software, are indeed available to everyone and generally affordable as a result of intense competition on a global level. What he failed to account for, however, is the difficulty in making all the disparate systems work together seamlessly. Achieving seamless integration is not easy, and those organizations that do it better than their competitors will indeed have an advantage. To say it differently, we need to return to the concept of information *systems,* not information *technology*. IT doesn't matter—but IS has never mattered more.

Integration is everywhere. Customers demand consistent treatment regardless of which channel they use, and they expect the organization to have all the information explaining them at their fingertips. Suppliers throughout the entire value chain are connected more tightly to your internal systems than ever before to meet the market demands. And senior executives are insisting on "one version of the truth" when it comes to customer information, market intelligence, and business performance measures.

If integration is so important, why does it have such a poor track record?
Consider these facts:

- The Standish Group, an information technology vendor who evaluates IT
  project and value performance, collects data every year on thousands of
  projects. Its 2003 survey shows that 15 percent of projects fail (never fin-
  ish), 51 percent are challenged (cost, schedule, or scope goals are not
  met), and only 34 percent are successful.

- The statistics for projects in excess of $10 million, which are by definition
  complex integration initiatives, are even worse: 39 percent fail, 60 percent
  are challenged, and only 1 percent fully succeed.

- A 2004 *Information Week* survey shows that 30 percent of companies that
  use ERP applications aren't buying new applications because they're too
  busy integrating the ones they already own.

- Integration challenges are cited as key factors in some highly publicized
  failures, such as the following:

  - Multiple breakdowns in the massive HP/Compaq IT integration resulted
    in an order backlog of $120 million.

  - ERP integration issues at Indiana University left students with no
    financial aid and required the university to dip into its reserve accounts
    in 2004.

  - The AT&T Wireless meltdown in 2003 was fueled by a botched
    customer relationship management (CRM) upgrade that cost the
    company thousands of new customers and an estimated $100 million
    in lost revenue.

Clearly, a poor integration track record puts your business operations and
market strategy at risk. In a few severe cases, large-scale IT failures have
put companies out of business. Conversely, if technology plays an important
role in your business and you are able to buy the best-of-breed components
and weave them together more seamlessly and at a lower cost than your
competitors, you will have a clear advantage. So how should you proceed?

2.5 The ICC Approach Is Different

A common knee-jerk reaction to these challenges is, "Let's buy all our software from one vendor, then the integration problem goes away." Many organizations attempted this in the 1990s and failed because:

- Buying from only one vendor requires taking the bad with the good; many business leaders are not prepared to make this drastic compromise.

- Mergers and acquisitions introduce redundant systems, which may take years to consolidate, if ever.

- The big ERP vendors are so big, and also grow by acquisitions, that they themselves have integration challenges.

- It is not cost beneficial to replace legacy systems and infrastructure every time a new technology emerges (typically every seven years), so most organizations have multiple generations of technology in use.

- Business-process outsourcing is driving organizations to contract with outside organizations to operate significant portions of the business, which often forces the use of the outsourcers' systems.

There must be a better way to integrate information systems in an adaptable and flexible way that doesn't constrain the business. Fortunately, there is—the ICC.

Fundamentally different from traditional project integration approaches, the ICC is based on the following principles:

1. Integration systems are distinct entities with their own life-cycle managed separately from application systems.

2. The "run" part of the life cycle is more important than the "build" phase— the emphasis is on adapting to change.

3. End-to-end business processes are modeled first, then applications are fit into the model.

4. Documentation is stored in structured (searchable) repositories with processes to maintain it (always current).

5. Solutions are based on open standards. Proprietary tools or "lock-in" methods are avoided to allow an exit path.

Chapter 4 will delve more deeply into these and other principles of an ICC and lay out the specific steps necessary to establish one.

2.6 Top 10 Reasons to Establish an ICC

There is no shortage of top-10 lists available from researchers and analysts; many offer "silver bullet" solutions. Unfortunately, there are no simple answers to complex issues, yet a top-10 list is a useful way to summarize this chapter. Here are our top 10 major reasons to establish an ICC:

1. **Enable disaster recovery.** Availability and continuity management are no longer simply about recovery systems; they involve recovering business processes. For example, if the mainframe is restored quickly after a disaster to enable the capture of orders, but the system that passes those orders on to the fulfillment system is not part of the disaster-recovery plan, then the order management process has not really been recovered. An ICC can ensure that end-to-end critical processes are understood and that all relevant touch points are recovered.

2. **Keep legacy systems alive.** This reason might sound negative, but the reality is that many legacy systems provide an adequate level of functionality and do not have a good justification to upgrade or replace them. Yet they need to be integrated with newer systems based on incompatible technologies. An ICC masks the differences and extends the value of legacy investments.

3. **Provide one version of the truth.** Few things are more frustrating to business executives (or damaging to the IT department's credibility) than conflicting information from fragmented IT systems. An ICC can help to resolve this problem by implementing disciplined approaches and effective technologies to keep the data in systems synchronized and build aggregate repositories, which act as the single source of business intelligence.

4. **Reduce complexity.** The common enemy is complexity, which in turn is caused not by large-scale quantities, but by large variations. An ICC can help to drive out variations by enforcing interface standards and data standards, thereby greatly reducing unnecessary complexity.

5. **Accelerate change.** Standardizing the middleware infrastructures and providing technologies to loosely couple systems enhance the ability of any component in the enterprise to change rapidly. This statement may seem counterintuitive, but adaptability, in fact, arises from structure.

6. **Boost team productivity.** Some people love dealing with infrastructure issues and being the "glue" that brings systems together, while others thrive on innovating within the scope of a specific business function. An ICC brings together the staff who really enjoy integration work and allows them to focus on what they do best.

7. **Eliminate surprises.** Disruptions to production operations can often occur because of an unknown dependency between systems. An ICC can help manage the release process to ensure that a simple change to one system doesn't cause problems with another system.

8. **Save money.** Enterprise efficiency is, of course, one of the main drivers for establishing an ICC. An ICC provides an enterprise focus: While the application teams focus on optimizing their system, the ICC focuses on optimizing the enterprise resources.

9. **Keep knowledge.** An effective metadata management strategy can allow an organization to hire consultants, do work offshore, and outsource selected business processes, yet still retain control over critical business and IT information.

10. **Facilitate regulatory compliance.** Believe it or not, George W. Bush signed the Enterprise Integration Act into law in 2002 (the legislation provides funding to research and promote integration practices). On a more serious note, a number of regulatory changes in recent years, such as the Sarbanes-Oxley Act, the Patriot Act, California Senate Act 1386, and various consumer privacy acts, place much higher demands on IT security and change disciplines. When integrations across an enterprise have fragmented management processes, it is very difficult to meet the regulatory demands. An ICC can be an effective way to meet the regulatory challenges.

Chapter 3

Starting an ICC

Because each type of ICC has its own advantages, organizations considering implementing an ICC should begin by defining the company's integration goals and the processes needed to accomplish them. Setting the goals and processes clarifies which type of ICC would be most appropriate and which roles and technologies it requires.

Starting an ICC that's right for your enterprise requires the development of an integration strategy. The challenge when starting from scratch, however, is similar to the proverbial "chicken and egg" problem: Should you develop the strategy first and then bring the resources on board, or should you establish the core leadership team first and let it develop the strategy? The answer is both: The integration strategy should involve an iterative process, with the executive sponsor driving a top-down process and the ICC team (once it is in place) building the bottom-up plan.

It's also possible that the ICC may be developed spontaneously as a grass-roots movement and grow organically. Only in hindsight does the organization recognize the ICC for what it is. In this scenario, the ICC team members may, in fact, be the best ones suited to document the strategy and gain formal management agreement.

Our recommended approach starts with a top-down strategy led by an executive sponsor. The executive sponsor starts with the presumption that integration is an enabler of the business strategy and that having a permanent part of the organization focused on integration as a discipline is a critical success factor. (Read Chapters 1 and 2 again if you're not ready to accept this statement as a baseline assumption.)

Although the integration strategy has many dimensions, we will focus here on the core issues related to people, process, and technology—in that order. But before we tackle any of these dimensions, we need to determine the organizational structure of the ICC. This structure describes the ICC's hierarchy within the organization and sets the foundation for how it relates to other parts of the enterprise. The structure will, to a large degree, drive the kind of people you need, the services they will provide, and the tools and technology they will need to perform them.

In a nutshell, establishing an ICC is a four-step process:

1. Select the ICC organizational model that's right for you.
2. Assemble the ICC team (people).
3. Determine your current and target integration practice maturity (process).
4. Develop the enterprise integration architecture (technology).

Of course, it's not this simple. The strategy needs to be reviewed and refreshed on a regular basis, and a number of other elements may be just as critical, including:

- Architecture principles
- Outsourcing strategy
- Financial policies
- Business alignment
- Supplier partnerships
- Standards selection

That said, the ICC organization model, including the people, the processes, and the technology considerations, is the base. Let's get started.

3.1 Step 1: Select the Organizational Model

There are five ways to organize an ICC, as Figure 3-1 shows. Each organizational model is defined by a particular profile of people, processes, and technology and results in a particular set of benefits to the organization. This book explains each of the dimensions and provides general advice on establishing an ICC.

	Project Silos	Best Practices	Standard Services	Shared Services	Central Services	Self-Service
Processes	Independent	Defined	Defined	Defined	Defined	Automatic
Technology	Independent	Recommended	Standardized	Standardized	Shared	Dynamic
Organization	Independent	Distributed	Distributed	Hybrid	Centralized	Invisible
Benefits	Innovation	Knowledge Leverage	Consistency	Resource Optimization	Control	Innovation & Efficiency

Figure 3-1. ICC Organizational Models

An integration competency center (ICC) supplies a number of advantages over traditional project teams working independently in silos. Although independent project teams may drive a great deal of innovation, that same innovation could be detrimental to the overall enterprise, which also needs to operate efficiently. Innovation in specific functional areas might be great, but variation in shared infrastructure adds complexity and cost.

There is not a single answer as to which organizational model is right for a given enterprise. First and foremost, however, clearly define the scope of your enterprise, and then ensure that whatever model you select, the ICC has an enterprisewide mandate for it.

3.1.1 Select the ICC Model That Meets Your Needs

ICCs are not all alike. They tend to fall into one of several categories: best practices, standard services, shared services, central services, or self-service. A best-practices ICC seeks to leverage knowledge by establishing and documenting effective integration processes. A standard-services ICC builds on the best-practices ICC but goes one step further, providing consistency by specifying the technologies to be used for all integration projects. A shared-services ICC incorporates the features of best-practices and standard-services ICCs and further optimizes use of resources by creating a shared environment for development, quality assurance (QA), and production. A central-services ICC is the most comprehensive type, providing enterprisewide control over integration activities by specifying best practices, setting technology standards, furnishing integration services, and assuming responsibility for some or all aspects of every integration project in the organization. A self-service ICC completes the picture by creating an environment that is sufficiently standardized and automated such that it becomes almost invisible from the perspective of the individual systems.

Each model is appropriate for a different set of business requirements, and a company might well evolve through the different types. For example, a company might first create a best-practices ICC. Following the ICC's success with a specific project, other groups might then start to follow the ICCs processes, choose to use the same technologies, or share the ICCs development environment. An organization might then decide to enforce the ICC's approach and even centralize all integration services within the ICC.

The following sections offer an overview of each of the ICC organizational models. Chapter 4 provides more details and discusses how to select the one that is best for your enterprise.

3.1.2 Best-Practices ICC

A best-practices ICC is the easiest to implement, which makes it a good first step for an organization that wants to begin leveraging integration expertise. This type of ICC focuses on establishing proven processes across business units. To achieve this goal, a best-practices ICC documents and distributes recommended operating procedures and standards for development, management, and mapping patterns. It also defines how to manage change within an integration project.

The primary function of this ICC model is to document best practices. It does not include a central support or development team to implement those standards across projects, and it might not include metadata. To implement a best-practices ICC, companies need a flexible development environment that supports diverse teams and that enables them to enhance and extend existing systems and processes. Such teams might be a subset of an existing enterprise architecture capability.

3.1.3 Standard-Services ICC

A standard-services ICC leverages knowledge as a best-practices ICC does, but it enforces technical consistency in software development and hardware choices. A standard-services ICC focuses on processes, including standardizing and enforcing naming conventions, establishing metadata standards, instituting change management procedures, and providing standards training. This type of ICC also reviews emerging technologies, selects vendors, and manages hardware and software systems.

A standard-services ICC standardizes all integration activities on a common platform and links repositories for optimized sharing of metadata. To support these activities, an ICC needs technologies that supply metadata management; enable maximum reuse of systems, processes, resources, and interfaces; and offer a robust repository, including embedded rules and relationships and a model for sharing metadata.

3.1.4 Shared-Services ICC

A shared-services ICC optimizes the efficiency of integration project teams by providing a common, supported technical environment and services ranging from development support all the way through to a help desk for projects in production. This type of ICC is significantly more complex than a best-practices or standard-services model. It establishes processes for knowledge management, including product training, standards enforcement, technology benchmarking, and metadata management, and it facilitates impact analysis, software quality, and effective use of developer resources across projects.

The team takes responsibility for the technical environment, including hardware and software procurement, architecture, migration, installation, upgrades, and compliance. The ICC is responsible for departmental cost allocation; for ensuring high levels of availability through careful capacity planning; and for security, including repository administration and disaster-recovery planning. The ICC also takes on the task of selecting and managing professional services vendors.

The shared-services ICC supports development activities, including performance and tuning. It provides QA, change management, release management, and documentation of shared objects. A shared-services ICC requires a shared environment for development, QA, and production. The environment must also include a global repository of shared objects, metadata reporting, and capabilities for version control.

3.1.5 Central-Services ICC

A central-services ICC controls integration across the enterprise. It carries out the same processes as the other models, but in addition usually has its own budget and a charge-back methodology. It also offers more support for development projects, providing management, development resources, data profiling, data quality, and unit testing. Because a central-services ICC is more involved in development activities than the other models, it requires a production operator and a data integration developer.

To achieve its goals, a central-services ICC needs a live and shared view of the entire production environment. Tools to maximize reuse of systems, processes, resources, and interfaces are essential, as is visibility into dependencies and assets. A central-services ICC depends on robust change, configuration, and release management; metadata management tools; and tools that enable the team to enhance and extend existing systems and processes. Also, because of the scope and scale of this type of ICC, vendors must offer more than a tool set: They need to be able to act as technology partners.

3.1.6 Self-Service ICC

The self-service ICC both achieves a highly efficient operation and furnishes an environment where innovation can flourish. To do so requires strict enforcement of a set of application integration standards through automated processes. Just as with the Internet, the self-service ICC has a number of tools and systems in place that support automated or semi-automated processes. Establishing a definitive software library is an important consideration here, as are self-service release management tools integrated with change and configuration management.

To a large degree, the self-service ICC becomes invisible to the project teams and system owners under normal operations. Here are just a few examples of how different roles interact with an ICC:

- Business analysts extract current-state process models from a repository and check them back in to the repository as future-state models. Consistency of the models is ensured through the use of common modeling tools, which enforce semantics and consistent notation conventions as well as automatic validation against an architectural reference model.

- Developers discover existing interfaces (services or message topics) by searching a registry of reusable software assets that includes detailed specifications of the interface, such as a Web Services Definition Language (WSDL) specification.

- Project managers schedule a release by submitting the proposed configuration changes to the release management system and receiving notification of the release date once all the appropriate approvals have been validated. A workflow system controls the approval and scheduling process, which the project manager can query at any time to find out where the request is in the process and if there are any roadblocks.

- Corporate audit reviews data privacy controls by generating custom queries against the metadata repository, which contains information about system data models, integration data models, security access logs, and data privacy settings.

There is not a lot of "rocket science" behind these scenarios from a technology perspective (although some sophistication in modeling and metadata tools is necessary). The bigger issue revolves around gaining agreement to a set of standards and governance processes. The role of a self-service ICC is to maintain strict control over a small set of standards concerning how applications interact with each other and over a core set of tools to automate the life-cycle processes around them.

3.2 Step 2: Assign the People

An ICC requires staff to take on certain roles to carry out its processes. The same person might take on more than one role — for example, a repository administrator might also serve as the metadata administrator, or the lead architect might also play the role of a developer.

Depending on the type of ICC and its size, a company might choose to allocate roles among a number of different teams. For example, an ICC might consist of an ETL project team and a data integration services team. The ETL project team would have responsibility for ETL project development, acceptance testing, deployment, and maintenance. It would include

ETL developer and data quality developer roles. The data integration services team would be responsible for the ETL environment: repository administration, architecture, processes, and procedures. It would include the roles of ETL architect, repository administrator, and metadata administrator.

Chapter 5 provides a detailed description of the roles with the various ICC models and other human-factor considerations.

3.3 Step 3: Determine the Processes

An ICC designs and implements processes for integration. Depending on staffing levels and ICC model, the ICC will either directly design and implement processes for a project or offer the project team documentation or consulting on design and implementation. ICCs usually establish three types of processes: standards, strategies, and procedures.

Standards are rules for sharing the data integration environment. They exist to facilitate the organization, identification, modification, and troubleshooting of project assets developed by several users operating in a shared environment. Some of the standards an ICC must set include standards for naming, methodology, and metadata.

Strategies are plans for achieving a desired goal. They offer project teams a broad range of available options and are adaptable to a specific project's needs. ICCs typically adopt strategies for handling frameworks, platform services, metadata, security, archives, communication, and other infrastructure needs.

Procedures are detailed how-to guidelines that spell out the tool-specific actions or tasks that implement the strategy. They might, for example, set out procedures for change management, metadata/documentation handling, production migration, and operational support.

Chapter 6 provides further details on ICC processes and the overall IT context within which they operate.

3.4 Step 4: Select the Technologies

Once you define your ICC's objectives and the roles to carry them out, you will have a clearer view of the technical capabilities needed. Most ICCs require technologies that provide a live, shared view of the entire production environment and that support maximum reuse of systems, processes, resources, and interfaces. Designers should be able to create, debug, and test transformation logic once and make it available for reuse across teams, projects, and different operating environments. This "define once, use everywhere" approach drives accuracy and delivers unmatched productivity.

A flexible, open software development kit (SDK) for developing connectivity with real-time and batch sources makes the ICC's work much easier. Essential features for the SDK include native access to system metadata, interpretation of system-specific data types, high-performance extraction and loading that leverages native system interfaces, and changed data capture.

Visibility into assets, including their configuration and dependencies, helps the ICC optimize performance, so for your ICC, you should seek tools that graphically present data flows and dependencies across all systems and processes to provide intelligent audit trails. You should also look for tools that offer a highly extensible and searchable directory of an enterprise's information assets.

Support for team-based development is critical for ICCs. Products must provide developers with check-in and -out object versioning, complete with a utility for comparing objects and robust reporting, so that multiple developers can share and manage groups of objects across teams, projects, and environments. Distributed development and global/local repository management ensure full reuse and control of objects and processes from one unified environment. Version control and object management enable teams to maintain multiple versions of an object, control development on the object, track changes, and use deployment groups to provide superior control and automation of deployment across environments and locations.

An ICC needs a fast and accurate way to coordinate technical and business metadata from leading data modeling tools, source and target database catalogs, and any repositories. It then requires a single, open repository to ensure that metadata is always up to date, complete, and available. The repository should be robust and include embedded rules, relationships, and a model for sharing data.

Diagnostic features help ICCs manage the changes to data structures and definitions that occur as data warehouses adapt to evolving business needs. These features should include the capability to validate data models, database catalogs, and other external metadata repositories for consistency. And when tools help the team identify inconsistent metadata, the team should be able to analyze the impact of a change and selectively refresh the repository as needed.

To enable the ICC to enhance and extend existing systems and processes and keep pace with growing infrastructure complexity, some industry leaders are implementing universal data services (UDS), a ubiquitous integration layer across the entire enterprise architecture. UDS supports the dynamic assembly of data services and can offer a set of flexible, easily deployed, and "smart" shared data services that help to eliminate data silos and simplify integration efforts, delivering consistent views of information across the organization. With this architecture, an ICC can extend the utility of existing systems without changing them, substantially reducing costs and business risks of integration.

To address scalability issues, most ICCs benefit from additional processing capacity on demand through server grid technology. Multiple servers connected to the same repository make up a grid that automatically balances workflow across the machines. With this capability, an ICC can efficiently use hardware resources across departments to spread the risk and cost of the data integration project.

Chapter 7 delves into the ICC technology issues in further detail.

3.5 How Will the CIO Know Whether the ICC Is Effective?

What measures can the CIO monitor to indicate that the competency center is being effective? Based on the principle that you can't manage what you can't measure, we are strong proponents of a metrics-based approach to managing an ICC and demonstrating its effectiveness to the CIO and the rest of the enterprise.

We will not focus here on traditional project-based metrics such as conformance to cost, schedule, or scope. Nor will we focus on traditional business case metrics, such as ROI, net present value (NPV), or payback of investment decisions. Granted, these measures are important for integration projects or infrastructure investments, but these proven techniques do not need to be repeated in this book.

Rather, our focus here is on an ongoing metrics-based practice with continuous improvement driven by defined service levels. At the risk of being overly obvious, in order to measure a service-level agreement (SLA), you first need to define the service, specify a level of service, and write it down in the form of an agreement. You might want to start off with a set of loosely defined services and capture some ad hoc metrics first; then once you have a clear picture of the processes and how to measure them, you would formalize them as an SLA. But whether the ICC services are loosely defined or not, always keep in mind who the customers are, what they value about the service, and how you would measure it. The key categories are:

- New capabilities (build)
- Support and operations (run)
- Informational metrics (manage)

Let's explore each area.

3.5.1 New Capabilities

New capability metrics are all about the design and build phases of the life cycle. These metrics apply primarily to the shared-services and central-services ICC, but some aspects of them also apply to other models. Key metrics are:

- **Change cost and coordination cost**—These metrics attempt to answer two questions: "For a given change to a single system, how many other systems are impacted?" and "What is the cost to coordinate and implement all the dependent changes?" Over time, a successful ICC should be able to demonstrate a more modular and loosely coupled architecture that results in lower costs for changes.

- **Cost and time to build an interface**—These metrics demand a clear definition of what an interface is, a way to determine levels of complexity, and a standard process that allows measurement of individual steps or the end-to-end process.

- **Defect rate during warranty period**—This quality metric can help identify whether integrations are being rushed into production prematurely or without adequate testing. Analyzing trends over time can be very useful to help influence future integration projects.

- **Software reuse and business data reuse**—Examples of this metric include the number of subscribers to a given published message, distinct clients accessing a given Web service, projects that have used the shared code framework, or data attributes that more than one XML schema uses. Many of these metrics may actually be more useful as ratios, such as the number of subscribers divided by the number of publishers.

- **Demand forecast**—This metric indicates the workload that is coming down the pipe for new integrations. An early warning indicator is needed to staff up resources in anticipation of demand.

- **Retirement rate**—This metric tracks the "death" part of the life cycle and is often the most overlooked area. New integration processes should explicitly seek production elements that can be turned off as a result of the new capability. If you set goals for retirement of hardware or software and recognize or reward staff for doing so, you might be surprised how much "junk" is cleaned up.

Once a baseline measure is in place, the ICC director should set improvement targets. For example, annual cost or time reductions of 50 percent are not uncommon in the first years of an ICC operation as repeatable processes are established, the staff becomes familiar with them, and the inefficiencies of traditional silo development are eliminated.

Most of these measures require some form of a time and cost accounting system. If the enterprise lacks a system that can capture and report on the information to support the above metrics, don't let that become a road-block. You can always create the ICC's own tracking system. Even a simple spreadsheet can work if the size of the team and the number of metrics are not too large.

3.5.2 Support and Operations

Support and operations metrics are focused on the "run" phases of the life cycle. These metrics are most appropriate for the central-services and self-service ICC models, but may also apply in other models. They are even more significant in enterprises that employ IT infrastructure library (ITIL) practices.

- **Incident response and resolution time**—This metric tracks the number of production incidents (usually defined by three or four levels of severity) that impact service levels. It also measures the time the incident occurred (or was detected), when a support team member responded to the notification, and when the service was returned to operation. The primary objective when a production incident occurs is to return operations to normal and meet defined service levels.

- **Problem resolution**—This metric is a companion to the incident metric; incident resolution focuses on restoring systems to an operational state, while problem resolution focuses on fixing systems permanently. These metrics include the number of incidents that are recurring and should aim to reduce the total number of incidents over time, measured as a ratio to the number of systems or number of integration elements.

- **Metadata completeness and quality**—These metrics focus on the number of information domains that are being captured as metadata, the completeness of each domain, and the accuracy of the information. These metrics are among the more challenging areas to measure, but here are a few practical examples: perform a daily scan (using automated tools) of all production servers to discover new or changed message queue elements that don't match the information in the metadata reposi-tory; have the help desk keep track of the number of times it queries the repository and can't find the system name given by the caller; compare the names of application staff in the repository (system owners, business owners, architects) with the HR database and flag any cases where the individual is no longer an active employee.

- **Performance, throughput, and response times**—These metrics measure production volumes and response times, or completion times for batch jobs, in relation to defined service levels.

- **Integration service availability**—This metric captures the percentage of time an integration service is available over a long time (such as months or years). It may focus on integration systems (such as data integration hubs) or on integration processes (such as customer data synchronization across multiple systems). If your organization is applying ITIL/ITSM SLA practices, then the ICC's services should be considered a key part of those metrics.

- **First-time release accuracy**—This metric is concerned with the causal linkage between defects in an initial release and incidents.

Two key aspects of measuring support and operations is to establish a reporting rhythm and to control trends over time. A weekly reporting period is fairly common, but every two weeks or monthly may be adequate in environments that are more stable and have less change. During critical production periods, daily reviews of operations reports may be appropriate.

3.5.3 Informational Metrics

Informational metrics focus on a variety of measures to help in planning and managing an ICC. Many of these are just as applicable to a best-practices ICC as they are to a self-service ICC. They may be useful for benchmarking your enterprise with others, comparing one area of your company with another, providing inputs for a multiyear strategy, justifying an investment business case, and implementing other forward-looking activities.

Recall that one of the prime purposes of the ICC is to get the integration hairball under control. Once all the interface dependencies between systems are known, and the information about them is current and up to date, then the battle to unravel the hairball is at least half over. Here are a few metrics that can help:

- **Application portfolio**—This metric counts the number of systems in the enterprise by category: business system, subsystem, integration system, and so on. (It may require collaboration with an enterprise architecture capability.)

- **Number of interfaces**—This metric tracks the number of interfaces by pattern, protocol, technology, and whatever other way you can think about counting them.

- **Project/Engagement statistics**—This metric counts the number of projects or customers that the ICC supports and their level of satisfaction with the work performed.

- **Standards exceptions**—This metric notes the number of exceptions that are made to approved standards, the number that are outstanding, and the number that have been resolved.

- **Staff certification statistics**—This metric measures the level of ICC staff skills, knowledge, and training. Modern demand management and IT portfolio management software are increasingly capable of managing this metric.

To wrap up the discussion on metrics, we should go back to the opening question in this section: What measures can the CIO monitor to indicate that the competency center is being effective? Any and all of the measures discussed in this section can help, but if we had to recommend just one metric, it would be reuse. Not only is reuse one of the strongest value propositions of an ICC, but it is also an indication of how well the team has anticipated and prepared for enterprisewide needs and how accepted the ICC is as a function.

3.6 ICC Case Studies

3.6.1 Best-Practices Case Study

A world leader in the design and development of cardiovascular medical products was laboriously re-creating similar integration solutions with different development teams. It had no common processes across its integration projects, no efficiencies of reuse, and a never-ending learning curve. The company sought to share expertise so that everyone didn't have to go through a lengthy learning process. It established a best-practices ICC that created a common development approach and proven processes for integration and reporting. Although the company's most experienced integration staff remained in their business units, they documented the best practices they had formulated, so that they could be leveraged across the organization. People across the company heard about the best practices and have since launched four new integration projects that use those processes to increase integration effectiveness. The shared-services ICC supports projects through a development help desk, estimation, architecture review, detailed design review, and system testing. It also supports cross-project integration through schedule management and impact analysis. When a project goes into production, the ICC helps resolve problems through an operations help desk and data validation. It monitors schedules and the delivery of operations metadata. It also manages change from migration to production, reviews change control, and supports process definition.

3.6.2 Standard-Services Case Study

Several business units at a large mutual fund and investment management firm needed a more effective way to integrate data from multiple sources. The business units recognized the value of having "gold" type copies of data. In preparing for this strategic endeavor, the company proactively created a centralized shared environment with Informatica. It dedicated three employees to supporting the shared environment and established team roles. The team then developed strategies, standards, and procedures for operating a shared environment. Although the team's first project took six months to complete, it finished more than 10 projects within the next six months. Created 18 months ago, the shared environment is the primary reason for significant cost savings and rapid implementation of projects that meet the business lines' integration needs. The team is reusing most of the integration processes and currently has almost 20 projects in production. The company believes that its integration competency center will continue to produce significant cost savings in the future.

3.6.3 Shared-Services Case Study

The supply chain integration project of a major car manufacturer required multiple teams and projects to share data and transformations. Although the projects had several source systems in common, the integration projects lacked a common approach, leading to considerable confusion and inefficiency. The company chose to resolve the problem by standardizing on Informatica, creating a best-practices methodology, and establishing a global metadata repository to share common objects across multiple projects. After achieving reuse of mapping objects (such as source mappings, target mappings, and transformations) in excess of 40 percent, the ICC promoted its services to other lines of business with data integration requirements. Currently, the company's ICC supports eight data integration projects and has achieved reuse of development work in excess of 30 percent across projects for a customer profile hub, a corporate customer data warehouse, global warranty claim processing, a vehicles data warehouse, order management, financial services, and financial reporting.

3.6.4 Central-Services Case Study

The integrated environment of a specialty retailer had become far too complex for any one person or group to understand all the dependencies. The company decided to create a central-services ICC to retain knowledge in a structured way and to strengthen the company's ability to leverage offshore resources. The company also valued the ICC's focus on processes—the source of its competitive advantage. The ICC is organized as a metrics-based practice with contractual service levels driving continuous improvement. Service-level agreements apply to new development, the reuse of software and data, and support and operations activities. The company gathers metrics on the application portfolio, the number of interfaces, project statistics, variances from the standard, and staff certification. The ICC enables the company to consistently deploy and manage Web services, reducing development cost and improving security measures and monitoring. The retailer has used its ICC frameworks for more than three dozen projects and saved more than $4 million to date.

Chapter 4

Road Map for Growth

4.1 Aligning the ICC with Enterprise Goals

A primary question to ask when developing an integration strategy is, "How good are we today and how good do we want to be?" To answer this two-part question, you need to assess your current organizational competencies, determine where you want to be on the competency spectrum, and set a goal for how quickly to get there.

To help answer the question, this chapter lays out seven competency areas related to effective integration and five maturity levels for each of the competencies. The seven integration competencies are:

1. Integration systems
2. Modeling management
3. Metadata management
4. Integration methodology
5. Business process management
6. Enterprise architecture
7. Financial management

Two of these, business-process management and financial management, are not entirely information services disciplines, but nonetheless are critical factors in how well the IT organization aligns with the business and in particular achieves higher levels of disciplines.

Each of the competencies has five levels of maturity:

1. Basic—Minimum level of professionalism that any organization should have
2. Mainstream—Proven best practices commonly found in many organizations
3. Advanced—Also proven practices, but less commonly found
4. Leading-edge—Look great on paper, but few real-life examples exist
5. Bleeding-edge—Paving new trails in uncharted territory

A sixth category, level zero, is pre-basic. Even the basic maturity level requires some disciplines, but they are so fundamental that we didn't bother defining a lower level. If your organization is not fully at level 1, make it a priority to address the gap before going any further. As with basic hygiene, it's a mandatory requirement.

Note that the terms used to characterize each of the levels are relative terms. A leading-edge practice today might be a mainstream practice in three to five years. The second law of integration, "There is no end state," applies equally to the disciplines and process of integration as it does to integrated solutions and to the technology in general.

As reflected in Figure 4-1, a key element of an enterprise strategy is the degree to which the organization believes integration is critical to achieving its business objectives.

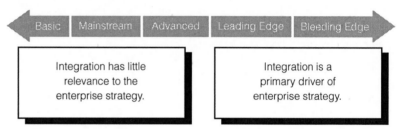

Figure 4-1. Integration Maturity and Enterprise Strategy

The question to ask is, "If we integrate our systems better, will it give the business a significant advantage?" If the answer is no, then you will likely not find a payoff in developing your integration maturity beyond level 2, mainstream. If the answer is yes, then the mainstream level should be the minimum level of competency at which you operate, and you would likely benefit from setting your target at advanced or leading edge. If a well-integrated environment is a *primary* driver of your advantage in the marketplace, then you will likely want to be near the leading edge with some efforts focused on bleeding-edge practices.

Going back to the opening question in this chapter, the maturity models offer a way to assess your organization's current level of capability and a framework in which to set an organizational goal related to how good you want to become. The third decision, how fast you intend to achieve the goal, is partly a factor of the ICC organizational model you select.

The following sections of this chapter describe the five levels of maturity for each of seven capabilities; but first, a few words about the relationship between maturity levels and ICC organizational models. Figure 4-2 identifies which maturity levels are relevant to which ICC models.

	Best Practices	Standard Services	Shared Services	Central Services	Self-Service
Basic	•	•			
Mainstream	•	•	•	•	
Advanced			•	•	•
Leading-edge			•	•	•
Bleeding-edge				•	•

Figure 4-2. Maturity Levels Versus ICC Organizational Model Matrix

Note that each column and each row has several options, but some combinations do not mix. For example, it would not make sense to go to the trouble of establishing a central-services ICC and implement only basic integration disciplines; a centrally managed pool of resources is overkill and would be counterproductive. It would also not be feasible to implement leading-edge practices in a best-practices model because the ICC is not likely to have either the staff or the technologies to effective drive the necessary enterprisewide disciplines. Finally, the bleeding-edge capabilities, by definition, require either a central-services or self-service ICC.

4.2 Setting Integration Maturity Goals

The maturity models described in this section are high-level checklists for quickly gauging your organizational maturity level and helping to set goals for the capability you want to achieve. These models are most commonly used as follows:

- **Step 1:** Perform a self-assessment of the organization's current maturity level—ideally based on the perspective of a number of staff from across the enterprise.

- **Step 2:** Set goals for the level of maturity you would like to achieve within a specific time (generally over a period of two to three years).

- **Step 3:** Develop tactical action plans to close the gap between the current state and the desired target state.

It is of critical importance to ensure that the seven maturity levels are in alignment and progress in unison. For example, if the business process management maturity is at level 3 while the metadata maturity is at level 1, this disparity will likely cause some conflicts. Before moving the business process maturity to a higher level, the metadata maturity must be brought to the same level. As a general rule, all maturity levels should be within one level of each other.

Finally, a word of caution: The maturity models are not a substitute for a detailed analysis of your organization's capabilities, nor do they include formal certification processes or industry benchmarks. For a detailed and complete assessment of your organization, refer to the extensive research literature available and hire industry analysts or experts when appropriate.

4.2.1 Integration Systems Maturity

Integration systems maturity focuses on the disciplines of interface design and development, and how advanced the organization is in managing interfaces as common shared infrastructure.

Maturity Level	Integration Systems
Basic	The most common interface pattern is the custom-built, point-to-point interface. Integration work occurs by direct collaboration between the systems being integrated, and the interfaces are regarded as an integral part of the business application rather than as a separate system. Interface documentation is stored in a central location.
Mainstream	Applications are decoupled through an abstraction layer and middleware technology so that changing one minimizes the effect on others. XML message formats are commonly used. A best-practices ICC promotes enterprise standards. Multiple teams use an enterprise shared-code framework for standard functions such as security access, database connectivity, and adapter development.
Advanced	Application interfaces are standardized across the enterprise. Integration systems for message-, service-, or process-based interfaces are designed and managed independently of individual applications. A shared-services ICC or central-services ICC is established, which enforces enterprise standards. Portal technologies supply end users with a common front end to most enterprise applications.
Leading-edge	The integration systems, whether message, service, or process based, include a business layer, which enables end users to directly monitor and control the operational interactions between systems. Users log in once, and a role-based authorization mechanism allows them to access any application in the enterprise without having to log in again.
Bleeding-edge	Applications are designed with an integration layer as an essential prerequisite. Integration requirements carry more weight than functional requirements in terms of product selection. A self-service ICC is established, and application infrastructure is considered a "utility" similar to the data network.

Figure 4-3. Integration Systems Maturity Model

4.2.2 Modeling Management Maturity

One of the challenges of integration is to make a complex system of systems easier to comprehend and understand. For this reason, abstraction and graphical visualizations are critical for an effective integration practice. Models are the primary language of integration and hence a critical dimension of an ICC.

Maturity Level	Modeling Management
Basic	Models are used regularly but without a formal discipline. Unified Modeling Language (UML) is used as a "sketching" language and notation conventions are not strictly followed. Models are developed using free-form tools such Word, Excel, or Visio to document requirements/designs and are aligned through manual processes.
Mainstream	Modeling notation and naming standards are defined, and teams across the enterprise use similar tools. Models are dynamic and stored as data in repositories rather than as static models. All staff members understand how to read UML (or equivalent) documents. Multisystem interactions are routinely modeled.
Advanced	Enterprisewide reference models are in place for business processes/functions, application architecture, information architecture (and data dictionary), and data-exchange or integration maps. Although the models might be stored in separate tools or repositories, it is possible to combine or link them through common keys and strict adherence to naming conventions.
Leading-edge	Models serve as "blueprints," with formal sign-off of business-process models and system design models before development begins. Transformation of models from one format to another occurs automatically using leading-edge tools with a common semantic integration standard.
Bleeding-edge	Simulators test requirements before design or development begins. Multiple future states are modeled and tools are used to identify and quantify impacts of planned changes. Model-driven architecture (MDA) concepts are used in conjunction with code generation tools to directly generate software.

Figure 4-4. Modeling Management Maturity Model

4.2.3 Metadata Management Maturity

The presence of an integration hairball indicates an integrated environment that is out of control. The issue is not the number of systems but their predictability and control. The ability to manage metadata, or data about anything in IT, is therefore an essential component of unraveling the hairball, because it allows you to understand all the dependencies and predict the impact of changes.

Maturity Level	Metadata Management
Basic	Metadata is generally thought of as "data about data" with little regard to capturing data about IT elements. Metadata management tools are used primarily by data management analysts or technical IT staff and are not considered a management tool.
Mainstream	A system inventory is maintained in a central repository and serves as the "official" list of applications in the enterprise. Each system receives a unique identifier (name), which is used consistently across the enterprise. Information about IT elements is captured generally using unstructured tools (such as Excel or Visio) and maintained through manual efforts.
Advanced	A metadata repository is in place that accurately reflects the data and integration dependencies in the production environment. Data definitions are based on a common data dictionary. There is a broad-based practice across the organization to capture data about IT elements (databases, servers, assets, incidents, and so on) and maintain it in a central repository. The metadata team collaborates with an IT service management/configuration management database (CMDB) team to unify all IT data.
Leading-edge	Metadata repositories model future states and perform systematic impact analysis and risk assessment on the current-state environment and changes to it. Scanning tools are used to automatically discover elements in production and changes to them. An enterprise integration model and enterprise data model are formally defined.
Bleeding-edge	A single unified (or federated) repository serves as the equivalent of an ERP for an IT database; it contains all relevant management information about IT processes, projects, systems, financials, assets, operations, services, and plans. Processes are in place to keep all the information current.

Figure 4-5. Metadata Management Maturity Model

4.2.4 Integration Methodology Maturity

An integration methodology is fundamentally different from a software engineering methodology. Software engineering techniques work fine for well-defined problems, but because integration is the process of making independent systems (possibly based on incompatible technologies) work together seamlessly, new techniques are necessary. An appropriate integration methodology recognizes the difference and compensates accordingly.

Maturity Level	Integration Methodology
Basic	Integration processes are dynamic and ad hoc, with success dependent on the efforts of competent and experienced individuals. Few integration processes are defined formally. Integration is generally viewed as a "project" activity and occurs during the development life cycle, with ad hoc maintenance on integrations once in production. Limited and focused change control, and change control is a gatekeeping function to production.
Mainstream	Integration processes are defined to identify cross-functional and cross-system impacts of planned changes early in the project life cycle. Basic integration metrics concerning cost, schedule, and requirements are tracked, and the discipline is in place to repeat earlier successes on integration initiatives with similar characteristics. Change control has evolved to change management.
Advanced	Integration management processes for the full life cycle are standardized, documented, and universally applied across the enterprise. A formal release process is defined and integrated with change and configuration management processes; it controls changes to applications across the enterprise. An ICC that is responsible for managing and optimizing integration systems in production is established.
Leading-edge	Continuous improvement is enabled by quantitative feedback from processes and from piloting innovative technologies. Internal and external data and process definitions are unified with common business functions supporting all channels.
Bleeding-edge	Integrated solutions are driven by business leaders with cross-functional or cross-channel enterprisewide responsibility; business measures of integration solution effectiveness are collected. Application systems or services operate as managed entities with enterprise governance around changes to public interfaces.

Figure 4-6. Integration Methodology Maturity Model

4.2.5 Business Process Management Maturity

Business process maturity mostly concerns the disciplines within the business areas and how consistently and formally the business process hierarchy is defined and managed. This maturity level is a critical factor in ensuring alignment between the IS organization and the business lines. A secondary factor of business process maturity is the degree of manual effort needed to keep the data in systems synchronized.

Maturity Level	Business-Process Management
Basic	Business processes are dynamic. They might not be fully documented, and even routine activities are highly people intensive. Replication of information across systems is through batch processes or is highly manual, with the same information being entered into multiple systems.
Mainstream	Business processes are documented and management processes are in place to monitor conformance and drive improvements within a functional area (but not necessarily cross-functionally). Replication of common information across systems is mostly automatic.
Advanced	Process modeling is done with standard language, stored in a repository, and monitored in production with basic monitoring tools. Business leaders actively participate in the integration life cycle and clearly see their role as part of the enterprise whole. Information is captured once at the source and flows to other systems in (near) real time.
Leading-edge	Business processes are measured by "process owners" in terms of time, cost, and effectiveness and are controlled using quantitative data. The focus is on a cross-functional process view. Information flow between applications and business units use business-process management (BPM) and business activity monitoring (BAM) tools and automated decisioning.
Bleeding-edge	Business processes are optimized through scientific principles, including controlled experimentation of new processes in production. Process simulation is practiced and BAM is used consistently regardless of the implementation mechanics of a process. A chief process officer has overall responsibility for continuous improvement of enterprise and supply-chain processes.

Figure 4-7. Business-Process Management Maturity Model

4.2.6 Enterprise Architecture Maturity

Enterprise architecture is arguably the most important of the seven capability areas. The architecture defines the structure and hierarchy, while the other disciplines focus more on doing the work. Without the structure of an effective enterprise architecture, the remaining six disciplines will have a hard time being effective.

Maturity Level	Enterprise Architecture
Basic	The role of a systems architect exists and is active at the project or program level. The effectiveness of a given architect is due largely to the skill and experience of the individual and not to any systematic processes. Cross-system architectural issues are resolved through ad hoc and informal processes. Technology standards are defined. "Enterprise" architecture may be mostly about technology selection; distinctions among functional, technical, process, application, and operations architectures are not well understood or organizationally delineated.
Mainstream	A formal, documented enterprise architecture exists, including definition of a reference framework for application systems and information subjects (in addition to technology standards). The enterprise architecture exists outside the context of a project or a program and is leveraged at the program and project level. Standard models are used to capture the systems architecture in a repository using enterprise architecture modeling tools. Distinction among more logical (business, process, function, application) and technical architectures is prevalent.
Advanced	The enterprise architecture includes a formal business architecture in addition to a system, information, and technology architecture. Business leaders are active participants in periodic (for example, annual) efforts to define architectural blueprints and multiyear road maps for the enterprise. An enterprisewide governance process is in place to ensure conformance to standards.
Leading-edge	Tight integration between business and IS is evidenced by a strong alignment between the architecture framework and the organizational structure. The business is modeled as a set of integrated capabilities. Organizational structures, processes, and systems are driven by business capabilities required to meet the business goals. Architects are formally held accountable for their designs and how they function in production. Projects are considered "done" only when exceptions to standards are resolved.
Bleeding-edge	Quantitative factors measure the flexibility and adaptability of architectural designs. Future technology risks and changes are quantified and included in annual planning processes and in project business cases.

Figure 4-8. Enterprise Architecture Maturity Model

4.2.7 Financial Management Maturity

Financial management maturity is primarily a process of senior management engagement and financial discipline. It is another critical factor in ensuring that the technology solutions align with the business plans and visions. Generally, maturity in this area can be measured through success with IT portfolio management as a functional area.

Maturity Level	Financial Management
Basic	Integration projects above a given cost threshold follow a standard process for business case justification that includes estimates of all project costs and benefits. Objective criteria are used to periodically assess the risks of large integration projects to provide early warning of threats to the realization of benefits.
Mainstream	The business case assumptions of large projects are incorporated into the budgets and performance targets of their business sponsors. An applications inventory is maintained and used to track costs by application and determine potential opportunities for retiring redundant systems.
Advanced	Project budgets take into account the costs of replacing redundant systems slated for retirement. Lessons learned from integration projects are codified for a central repository and used to improve future estimate accuracy and process execution. A product/service catalog is available that provides end users with "plain English" descriptions of specific IT services and their cost drivers. Costing occurs at the services level. Service models include base services and incremental discretionary services driven by strategy and tactical demands.
Leading-edge	The organization conducts reviews after implementation to measure achievement of project benefits. IT maintenance resources are prioritized based on an applications business value, revenue impact, and geographical scope. The IT organization conducts periodic benchmarking of development and operational cost efficiency.
Bleeding-edge	IT business cases include explicit factors that quantitatively weigh the degree of flexibility available from the architecture for adapting to business changes and project risks. Business sponsors are encouraged to proactively terminate projects for which there no longer remains a sound business case.

Figure 4-9. Financial Management Maturity Model

4.3 Defining Integration Principles

Integration principles capture a core set of beliefs about what an organization values in developing a comprehensive practice for enterprise integration. Principles, in general, have the following characteristics:

- Declarative
- State a belief
- Influence behavior
- Filter choices
- Focus on guiding change

An organization could adopt a wide range of integration principles. The 10 integration principles listed below are commonly found in organizations that have an established ICC and a strong enterprise architecture practice. Some advice to consider as you create your own set of integration principles:

- Too many principles are difficult to remember. Try to select no more than five.

- Once yesterday's principle becomes generally accepted, there is no point in stating the obvious.

- Only new or controversial principles are worthy of emphasis.

Finally, keep in mind that creating principles for an enterprise is as important as the final result. Gaining input from a cross-section of the IT organization and building a consensus about how to interpret the principles are critical aspects of adopting an effective set of guiding principles.

4.3.1 Principle 1: Loosely Coupled, Tightly Integrated

This principle may seem like a contradiction in terms, but it is at the heart of an ICC organization's purpose. The intent of this principle is to loosely couple systems so that a change to one system will have a minimal impact on the others, yet recognize the explicit dependencies among them. This principle implies that there is a common approach for integration across the enterprise, which preferably is formalized as a written statement of enterprise integration strategy.

The scale and complexity of all the information systems and operations demand that the work be divided up into smaller parts using diverse technology that is managed by separate groups—yet all the parts must work together seamlessly. Users (whether internal or external customers) have every right to expect a consistent level of service, including performance, reliability, security, scalability, and simplicity. A unified and comprehensive integration approach ensures that different groups can focus on specific components while still optimizing systems and operations across the enterprise.

Some implications of this principle:

- Consistent standards must be followed even when IT responsibility is decentralized. By definition, individual IT groups are not autonomous and must conform to integration standards.

- The integration architecture must encompass the entire "work architecture": process models, business events, transaction data, shared data model, and so forth.

- Application systems must be clearly identifiable in terms of management responsibility and the application's components (that is, you should be able to draw a box around them). The application architecture governs components inside the box, while the "integration architecture" governs the space between the boxes.

- Every project proposal or plan should clearly identify application costs and integration costs.

4.3.2 Principle 2: Limit Integration Options

A common approach is essential to reduce the proliferation of point-to-point interfaces and integration complexity. The organization must choose the smallest set of integration technologies that satisfies the spectrum of needs in an acceptable manner and is manageable from an operational and support perspective.

Integration between applications is a shared infrastructure that can and should be optimized across the enterprise. More than 500 middleware vendors offer integration products. Although many of the products are excellent, an organization simply cannot support them all at a practical level.

Implications:

- Projects must choose between specifically defined integration options. If the defined options don't meet the need, a formal process must be followed to evaluate, select, and adopt a new enterprise standard to fill the need; the project team can't just decide on its own.

- For a given application or project, the limited choices might not be ideal. Optimizing the whole system implies that at least some subsystems will be less than optimal; trade-offs are a fact of life.

- If a project deviates from the standard (for time to market or other reasons), the project must bear the cost of retrofitting to the standard and will not be considered "done" before doing so.

4.3.3 Principle 3: Use a Process-Driven Cross-Functional Approach for End-to-End Solutions

As part of the selection, design, and implementation of IT solutions, the technology and business teams must work together to ensure that IT components are defined in terms of their role in the end-to-end business processes.

There are many dimensions to integration, including data, systems, processes, platform, operations, business unit, and geography. Although all dimensions are critical, it is necessary to choose one as the anchor point for beginning problem analysis, modeling solutions, and driving changes. The key benefit from integration is not simply creation of a collection of interfaces, but also provision of service to all business operations and ultimately the entire supply chain. In this regard, the business process dominates and drives value to the enterprise.

Implications:

- The organization needs an enterprisewide methodology for describing and modeling end-to-end business processes.

- Interfaces need to be associated with the business processes they support.

- The failure of a given integration component should be analyzed from the standpoint of the business processes it impacts.

- Capturing the metadata associated with the business process and associated data is critical.

- It is necessary to clearly identify owners within the business who have management responsibility for end-to-end processes.

4.3.4 Principle 4: Integration Is as Important as Functional Requirements

Broadly speaking, an application must support being integrated with other applications. This principle states that integration requirements are a mandatory consideration for application selection/design and are a prerequisite before considering functional requirements.

Applications that do not satisfy certain minimal requirements to make them play well with others will be more trouble than they are worth. A truly stand-alone application in today's IT environment is rare—applications are all connected in some way. When the connections are through a common shared infrastructure, then the integration requirements become essential to the effectiveness of the application.

Implications:

- Software components (applications, adapters, transports) should be modular and accessed through simple public interfaces. They should be event driven and support a degree of separation between business processes and functions/data.

- Application systems must support enterprisewide functionality, serving all brands and channels and encompassing both internal and external communications. Services must be attached to the enterprise bus as shareable business domain services.

- Single-function applications that satisfy a clear business need are preferable to amorphous multifunction software applications. Eliminate redundant functionality whenever possible. Multifunction business applications frustrate the ability to eliminate redundancy.

- Formal integration requirements need to be created and agreed on by all application teams. The API should be based on the Web services descriptive language (WSDL), row address strobe (RAS), or Java metadata interface (JMI) to enable dynamic service discovery, metadata interchange, and tool exit strategies. For example, all applications, whether purchased or built, must be:
  - Able to run without a graphical user interface (GUI)
  - Capable of being accessed through an API
  - Business event driven and controllable through an external workflow tool

- Packaged applications should be accessed only through defined integration points. This feature will allow the package to evolve with minimal impact on other applications. In particular, avoid customizing applications from external vendors.

- Enhance packaged applications by extension (bolt-ons), not by internal modifications.

4.3.5 Principle 5: Reuse Before Buy, Buy Before Build

The first priority is to use, and reuse, software assets that already exist in the enterprise. Unlike other assets such as hardware, people, facilities, and money, software has a unique property that allows it to be reused an infinite number of times without consuming the original (within licensing constraints, of course). The second choice is to buy application systems, and only as a last resort should an application be built from scratch.

One of the implications of this principle is that it might drive the emphasis of in-house software development away from application systems development and toward integration systems development. Most IT shops will find that even with a strong "buy" philosophy, they will still have a large staff of software engineers and spend considerable effort on the "glue" that binds the systems together. From this perspective, the principle of "buy versus build" might not be relevant and might be replaced by the principle of "buy and build."

A case can be made that sophisticated frameworks such as .NET and Java Struts, coupled with patterns and agile methods, are making "build" a much more practical and realistic approach, by abstracting a great deal of plumbing and allowing much more business value-add work by the software engineer. This approach results in specific business functionality and corresponding competitive advantage.

4.3.6 Principle 6: Unify Architecture Management

The planning and management of the enterprise architecture must be unified with consistent standards, even when IT responsibility is decentralized. This principle must apply to all processes for funding, review, and approval of technology/development efforts.

The architecture should apply to the entire enterprise and should be coarse-grained to provide sufficient consistency at a high level for interoperability while allowing a certain degree of local freedom. For example, the architecture should support semantic diversity (different interpretations of the same data) and permit diversity in the use of technical tools and techniques. Where to draw the line between enforced standards and individual choice is a matter of enterprise culture and policy.

The architecture should also provide the basis for organizational responsibility and ownership for each of the layers.

4.3.7 Principle 7: Consolidate First, Integrate Second

A goal of the enterprise is to reduce integration complexity through standards, standard products, and consolidation of similar applications into single systems.

Just because we can integrate independent systems doesn't mean that it should be the first choice for developing business solutions. Integration adds overhead and additional layers of complexity that should be avoided when possible. The first choice, whenever feasible, should be to consolidate disparate systems that perform similar functions into a single system.

A common cause of fragmented and overlapping systems in organizations today is the result of different parts of a company building their own system and duplicating functions that other parts of the company also perform. This situation is especially true in the case of separate companies that merge. Over time, this redundancy can lead to extreme fragmentation and overlapping functionality in corporate applications. To prevent this problem, organizations need to adopt a stronger, even ruthless, predisposition to consolidate system components and increase reuse across the enterprise.

The proliferation of systems creates what is often called "the N_ problem." The phenomenon occurs with both systems and people: As the number of elements (N) that need to interact increases, the lines of communication increase exponentially. The formula for this model is (N_ - N) / 2 and it appears graphically below.

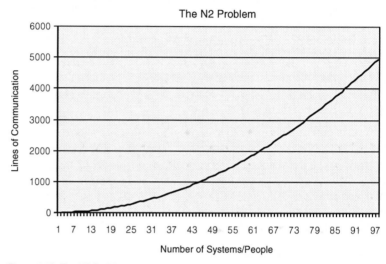

Figure 4-10. The N2 Problem

Simplifying an IT environment by consolidating redundant systems based on this dynamic results in significant benefits. For example, in an enterprise with 100 systems, reducing the number of systems by 25 percent would result in a 44 percent reduction in complexity.

You can reduce complexity by either physical consolidation (converting data and processes from one system to another) or logical consolidation (grouping similar systems together under common management). Just as an organizational hierarchy helps manage the communication lines among many people, an application hierarchy makes increasingly complex systems more manageable.

4.3.8 Principle 8: Develop a Common Representation of Data and Process

The goal of this principle is to create an interchange language that is common to all applications within the enterprise, generic enough to be decoupled from any given application, and robust enough to represent the necessary data and process information for any given application. This representation would facilitate communication among the various applications because they would all "speak the same language."

Many efforts are under way in various industry segments to gain agreement on common definitions of data and process elements. Some industry segments have progressed further than others. For example, the manufacturing industry has STEP (standard for the exchange of product data), which can be used to exchange product models among CAD (computer-aided design) systems. And various industry bodies led by the National Institute of Standards and Technology are working on a process specification language (PSL) to permit the interchange of models between different manufacturing processes.

It is not clear when, if ever, we will have a truly universal, industry-neutral interchange language. In the meantime, each enterprise will need to develop its own common language, preferably in collaboration with standards bodies within their own industry segment.

4.3.9 Principle 9: Manage Integration Systems as Distinct Entities

Interfaces between application systems are considered part of the enterprise's shared infrastructure rather than being part of one or both of the application systems. Collectively, all the interfaces are treated as one or more integration systems, which are managed as distinct entities with their own life cycle.

One implication of this principle is that point-to-point interfaces, which in the past were developed and maintained by an application team, might become the responsibility of a central-services or self-service ICC. The ICC would have the mandate to seize control of interfaces and retrofit them in the interests of the enterprise.

4.3.10 Principle 10: Refactor Interfaces Constantly

A stable interface is a key to sustaining quality integrations, yet there is no stability in applications, protocols, standards, or technology, producing a dilemma. Recall that "legacy" software is based on a prior generation of technology. This principle addresses the dilemma by asserting that interface software must be constantly refactored as an organization adopts new technology.

Following this idea further, and based on the assumption that no organization has unlimited funds to constantly rewrite interface software, we conclude that a somewhat different approach is needed: specifically, a flexible, extensible, component framework that is applied consistently throughout the enterprise. As the framework is extended and modified by the various integration initiatives, the changes are rolled back into the common framework. This idea is similar to the "open software" concept where everyone has access to the source code and may change it on the condition that all changes must conform to certain standards and be incorporated into the base.

Extreme programming (XP) is an approach to software development based on several practices that are particularly well suited to interface development. The relevant core practices are:

- Users define requirements through stories/scenarios.
- XP teams use a common system of names and descriptions.
- Developers write automated unit tests first, then the code.
- The overall code design is frequently revised and edited by developers (refactoring).
- All programmers have collective ownership of the code base.
- Everyone must follow a common coding standard so all the code looks as if it were written by a single individual.

Ultimately, once certain performance and technical problems are solved, we would have interface elements that are self-testing, publicly registered, automatically discovered, and dynamically bound at runtime. This approach would not eliminate the need to constantly refactor software, but it would address a major issue related to configuration management.

4.4 Eliminate the Integration Hairball

The term "integration hairball" was first used by one of us (John Schmidt) in 2001 to describe an out-of-control situation resulting from poorly understood interface relationships between application systems. Since then, the term has become a widely used shorthand for overly complex and unmanageable system dependencies. The implications of a hairball include high cost of change, unpredictable operations, and long repair time.

Most large organizations have a hairball. The reasons include continual technology changes, different standards used by independent project teams, the lack of an overarching enterprise architecture, a system-centric rather than business-process-centric implementation methodology, mergers and acquisitions, and poor documentation of changes that occur over time.

Note that what creates a hairball is not simply a large number of interfaces; rather, it is caused by undocumented and poorly understood interfaces that result in production "surprises." The ability to inventory and document interfaces in a systematic and sustainable fashion is the first step to unraveling the hairball.

Remember that the hairball refers not to the interfaces within a system but rather to the interfaces between systems. We assume that individual systems are strictly engineered according to a standard imposed by a single architect. Systems integration, in contrast, is the process of making applications that were independently developed (possibly with different technology) and managed work together.

4.4.1 How Big Is Your Hairball?

Before answering this question, be sure you clearly understand both "system" and "interface." A system is a logical construct used to simplify complex technologies. It is a means of grouping physical, executable components in service of a particular business or technical purpose. A given system can have tens or thousands of physical components. System types include the following:

- **Business system:** Supports a particular business function or process.

- **External system:** Is managed by an outside entity such as an application service provider (ASP).

- **Infrastructure system:** May be shared by many business systems, such as lightweight directory access protocol (LDAP) or domain name services (DNS).

- **Integration system:** Integrates data, such as a data warehouse, an operational data store, or a message broker.

- **Subsystem:** A logical, smaller part of a system that may operate or evolve independently from other parts of the system.

Because systems are logical groupings subject to interpretation, there is no "right" number of systems for a given enterprise; the "right" number is the one to which everyone agrees. The first step to sizing your enterprise hairball is to categorize and inventory all your systems. This inventory is called an *application portfolio*. Because the application portfolio is always changing, this chore is not a one-time effort. Critically, this work must be done from a holistic, companywide perspective, and it must be maintained in a repository systematically.

Systems exchange data. This exchange is often depicted as follows:

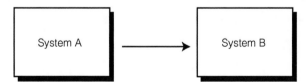

Figure 4-11. System Interface

Often there may be many feeds between two systems. Different data topics and different technical infrastructures may require a depiction looking more like Figure 4-12:

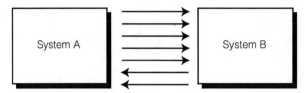

Figure 4-12. Two-Way System Interface

Note that data is flowing in both directions. Each interface may use a different technology, be managed by different teams, flow through different servers, use different protocols, and be controlled by different operational tools.

Counting interfaces is therefore deceptively complex, and since there are no industry standards in this area, we must be careful. For example, how should we count physical versus logical interfaces? If system B runs on a server farm, where each server is capable of interfacing with system A, should the number of interfaces be multiplied by the number of servers? And what if each server has multiple instances of the application executing on it? And how should interfaces between two business systems be counted when they flow through an integration system? Without industry standards in this regard, each organization must create its own metrics.

The number of physical interfaces is much larger than the number of logical interfaces. Still, both present unique challenges: a high number of physical interfaces present an operational challenge, and a high number of logical interfaces present an application management, documentation, and data-mapping challenge.

As the saying goes, "You can't manage what you can't measure." The first step toward eliminating the hairball is developing a sustainable application portfolio and conducting an inventory of interfaces and the dependencies between them.

4.4.2 How Do You Know When the Hairball Is Gone?

Identifying and effectively controlling interfaces is necessary but insufficient. A tougher question is, "What is the most efficient way to integrate applications resulting in the fewest number of discrete interfaces, and how can we measure success?"

A point-to-point integration pattern is efficient when only two systems use the same information. A publish/subscribe pattern is more efficient when two or more subscriber systems can take advantage of the same published information. Other integration patterns, such as a service oriented architecture (SOA), are most efficient when many systems in the enterprise need access to a common executable business function.

One of the intrinsic measures of middleware value is the degree to which you can reuse an interface. To measure reuse, assume that each topic is created by a project, and therefore only one use of the topic is expected:

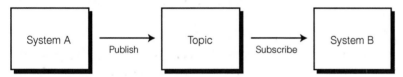

Figure 4-13. Single Middleware Subscriber

Additional uses (for example, to system C below) increase value, as Figure 4-14 shows.

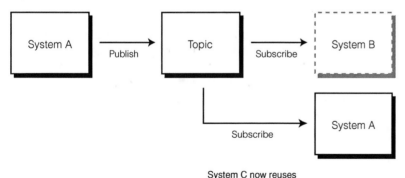

System C now reuses

Figure 4-14. Multiple Middleware Subscribers

In the first example (see Figure 4-13), reuse is 0 percent. In the second example, reuse is 100 percent. When a large number of publish/subscribe interfaces are aggregated, the result is an average reuse measure.

No accepted industry benchmarks exist for what is considered a "good" level of reuse for middleware. Common sense would suggest that 100 percent should be the minimum target, so that, on average, each published topic is used by two other systems. This target is based on the assumption that we would not bother to translate the interface data into a generic format if only one system were to use that data. If that were the case, we could employ simpler point-to-point interfaces. A more desirable target might be 200 percent reuse, meaning that three systems use each published data topic. How can we get rid of the hairball?

Eliminating the integration hairball in any large organization is a multiyear journey. Remember, the point is to eliminate the hairball in a sustainable fashion and not as a one-time Herculean effort. Establishing core processes and training a broad spectrum of staff across the IT organization is a major change management initiative and should not be underestimated.

The following key initiatives will, if sustained, unravel the integration hairball, replacing it with a high-performance IT operation that responds to business needs quickly and at a low total cost of ownership:

- **Application portfolio**—An inventory of applications across the enterprise and who is responsible for them. The portfolio must be maintained in a managed repository with sufficient disciplined processes in place to ensure that it always reflects the current reality. An organizational change (splitting one business unit into two, for example) can result in a redefinition of existing systems—even if none of the systems is changed physically.

- **Metadata repository**—A central metadata repository, such as that provided by Informatica, containing the integration metadata based on a formal data model. The repository may also contain metadata about business data (the data warehouse, for example), but more important, it contains information about hardware assets, processes, software components, and the relationships among all of them. It may also be tightly linked with a CMDB or with other operational systems that manage incidents, problems, releases, and so on.

- **Manageware**—A set of systems that manage operations, security, and changes to the infrastructure. Examples include Nastel for WMQ message-based interfaces and Amberpoint for Web services interfaces. These tools should interact with the metadata repository to keep the integration meta-data current and may be supplemented with scanning tools and adapters that continuously monitor the production environment and automatically update the repository.

- **Frameworks**—A Java or .NET (or both) software framework that developers can use to perform common services. Every interface in an enterprise should have a consistent way of handling security, logging, event notification, operational commands, database connection, registration, discovery, and deployment. It is not enough to give development teams guidelines for these critical aspects—the enterprise must invest in developing and maintaining a common framework that everyone uses.

- **Enterprise standards**—A set of documents and tools defining the rules that everyone must follow and a governance process to ensure that they stay current and relevant. The best way to enforce standards is not only to write them down but also to build them into daily processes and procedures. It's about time the IT department used more workflow and BPM tools to do its work.

- **Industry standards**—This is where the work of the Integration Consortium, The Open Group, the OMG, and other standards organizations is so critical. But end-user organizations need to be more actively involved, and the responsibility for setting standards cannot be abdicated to software vendors. Only by taking a strong leadership role in standards initiatives and partnering with software vendors can you unravel the hairball in a sustainable way.

These initiatives will not be successful unless someone is willing to champion and own them. Organizations must have a strong ICC to drive the initiatives and an architectural governance process to ensure that everyone plays by the rules.

Once all of these initiatives have been successfully established (which could take two to five years), a breakthrough occurs: The need for a strong, central integration development group disappears. At that point, no one "owns" the integration bus, and everyone can use and improve it. The result is a sustained low-cost infrastructure and continuous innovation. This result is what has made the Internet so successful. First, we must get everyone to play by a minimum set of application integration standards.

And *that's* how to unravel the hairball.

4.5 The Business Value Proposition

The business value of an ICC generally falls into one or more of several categories: efficiency, flexibility, stability, or revenue growth.

Efficiency means reducing costs and eliminating waste in IT operations, but it can also have a significant multiplier effect across the entire enterprise. For example, consolidating redundant customer systems may reduce IT operating costs by millions of dollars per year, but the cost savings could be 10 times larger once the simplification effects across thousands of call-center staff are taken into consideration. Our primary advice is to not limit the potential scope of influence of the ICC to only IT costs; consider how it can enable the whole enterprise, and even the entire supply chain, to operate more efficiently.

Flexibility involves enabling rapid time to market (or time to production) of new functionality. Loose coupling of systems is a key driver by allowing one system to change in response to a business need without the need to coordinate and synchronize the change with other systems. Flexibility also concerns supporting evolutionary changes rather than revolutionary changes of processes and functions. For example, if the enterprise wants to roll out new workstation software for its 10,000 front-office staff, it should be able to do so incrementally and gradually over a period of months (or years) without having to maintain duplicate back-office systems. The middleware infrastructures should accommodate this sort of flexibility.

Stability is about predictability and control of the production environment. Predictability is a factor of complexity, which is in turn a factor of variation and rate of change, so if your enterprise has a high rate of change and demands a consistent user experience, then providing a stable operating platform may be one of the biggest value propositions of the ICC. For example, if the enterprise's primary customer channel is the Internet, which demands consistent 24x7 access to information contained in a network of systems in the supply chain that change constantly, a strong ICC effort to control changes in the environment would be of great value to the business.

Revenue growth can also be a big motivator to establish a strong ICC. For example, building a consolidated view of the customer from fragmented and disparate systems to cross-sell products or services can be huge source of new revenue for an enterprise. Let's say the marketing department wants a totally new view of the 1,000+ tables in the data warehouse; rather than a product orientation, the company wants a customer segment view of all the information as well. By leveraging an ETL system that is driven by well-maintained metadata definitions, an ICC may be able to generate the new views in weeks rather than in months or years.

Here are suggestions about managing the value proposition of an ICC that have been demonstrated to be successful in the past.

- Use an internal, fixed-price, project charge-back scheme to keep management of integration funds separate from project management. This system can help avoid situations where a project team on a tight budget compromises the interface standards by cutting corners.

- When an ICC is first established, there may be a negative perception around the high cost of integrating systems because the costs of integration will become visible for the first time. The best advice to counter this perception is to collect and communicate benchmark information as best you can; in time, if the ICC is being effective, costs will start to come down.

- Don't charge the first project with the full cost of building an enterprise shared infrastructure. Seek out funding sources within the enterprise to make infrastructure investments before the projects need it. You may have to take the proposals to a high senior level in the enterprise to find someone who understands the big picture, can operate strategically, and is truly motivated to address the long-term issues.

- Do some internal marketing by telling stories about specific successes. Broad-based metrics are fine as well, but specific stories about customer situations, operational efficiencies, performance improvements, and successes of individual efforts are a great way to make the value of an ICC more "real" to people.

4.5.1 Example: ETL and Metadata Efficiencies

Informatica Professional Services conducted a survey of 50 non-ICC customer projects in 2003. The results of that survey showed that, on average, a data integration project cost $500,000, took 270 person-days, and required more than 200 mappings to complete. Assuming a 35 percent reuse of development work from one project to the next over an average of 10 projects (which is a very defendable assumption), the cost savings to an enterprise for deploying an ICC are extraordinary:

- Reduction in development cost:
  $500,000 x 10 projects x 35 percent = $1.75 million

- Reduction in project lead time:
  270 person-days x 10 projects x 35 percent = 945 days

- Reduction in maintenance cost:
  200 mappings x 10 projects x 35 percent = 700 mappings

4.5.2 Example: Server Consolidation

A leading-edge Fortune 100 company was an early adopter of middleware technology in the late 1990s. The implementations, however, were done by project teams operating in silos, which ended up deploying many message-broker servers. One of the first tasks the ICC took on when it was established was to inventory all the message brokers; 21 production servers were discovered. After conducting some performance analysis and capacity planning, the team figured that it could handle the peak business volumes with just 12 servers. The workload was consolidated with zero production incidents and the company is saving more than $300,000 per year (9 servers x $30,000 average cost per year to lease and support each server, plus additional application support costs, add up to more than $300,000 annually).

Chapter 5

ICC People

Finding the right people to staff an ICC is not easy. Integration as a discipline is a new practice, which means that if you are setting up an ICC for the first time, chances are that you won't have many (or any) staff in your enterprise who have direct experience working in this mode.

Clearly, many of the technical, communication, and management skills that people may have developed working in other IT functions are also applicable to an ICC. For example, program management, quality assurance, enterprise architecture, software development, data modeling, and other disciplines are all critical ingredients of an integration team. But while these skills are necessary, they are not sufficient. Just because individuals have a track record of success working in a specific function or on a project team won't guarantee their success in an ICC.

These three additional factors determine how successful a person will be on an ICC team:

- **Capacity to think outside the box.** The best people are those who don't see a box at all. Integration is about bringing disparate and disconnected elements together, so the ICC practitioner should be willing and able to think in the broadest-possible terms. While a given integration task may simply involve connecting two systems together, the ICC staff should ask: *What are those systems connected to? What are the upstream and downstream impacts? What about the customers of the customers and the suppliers of the suppliers?* Look for people who can see the big picture, yet stay focused on the immediate task at hand.

- **Capability to play a facilitator role.** Although analytical skills are absolutely necessary, they are often insufficient to develop the "right" answer in an integrated environment. The "right" answer is often the one that everyone agrees with rather than one based on some notion of theoretical purity—hence the need for the ICC staff to often act as mediators. Look for people with a strong customer service orientation who can listen well, appreciate both sides of a story, and find the common ground among diverse perspectives.

- **Ability to act as a change agent.** Don't underestimate how significant a change the ICC approach is compared with the traditional silo organizational model. ICCs demand a fundamental shift in responsibility from application teams who have traditionally designed and built the interfaces for the system(s) they own to a model where interfaces are treated like a shared infrastructure. The key advice is to find people who are persistent and don't need a well-defined path to achieve a goal. Section 5.3 offers more on this important topic.

5.1 Each ICC Model Requires Different Roles

The following chart lists the most common roles within each of the five ICC models.

	Best Practices	Standard Services	Shared Services	Central Services	Self-Service
Change Control Coordinator			•	•	•
Data Integration Architect			•	•	
Engagement Manager				•	
ICC Director			•	•	
Integration Business Analyst			•	•	•
Integration Developer			•	•	
Knowledge Coordinator	•	•	•	•	•
Metadata Administrator	•	•	•	•	•
Product Specialist				•	
Production Operator				•	
Project Manager			•	•	
Quality Assurance Manager			•	•	
Repository Administrator				•	•
Security Administrator				•	•
Standards Analyst		•	•	•	
Technical Architect			•	•	•
Technology Leader		•	•		•
Training Coordinator	•	•	•	•	•
Vendor Manager		•	•	•	•

Figure 5-1. ICC Staff Matrix

Note that only two of the roles, knowledge coordinator and training coordinator, cut across all organizational models. If you haven't decided which model is right for your organization, start by filling these roles, because you'll need them in any event.

The list of roles in Figure 5-1 is neither complete nor comprehensive, but it should be sufficient to get you started. Feel free to mix and match the roles as it makes sense for your enterprise, and don't feel constrained to stick with the matrix too literally.

Our general recommendation is to grow the ICC over several years rather than overnight because it takes time to find the right staff, develop their skills and experience, and mature the enterprise standards and best practices. The normal trend is to move from left to right on the ICC model chart: Start with a few people in a best-practices ICC, expand it to the standard-services ICC with a strong emphasis on governance, begin to pool resources in a center of expertise (COE) under the shared-services model, assume full life-cycle responsibility in a central-services model, and ultimately disperse the team to the rest of the organization and downsize to a smaller core group in the self-service model.

That said, how fast you move through the ICC life cycle, whether or not you leapfrog some phases, or whether you decide to stop at some point and not strive for the self-service model, is all a matter of company culture and your enterprise integration strategy.

5.2 Staff the ICC with the Right People

Of the three dimensions—people, process, and technology—the people dimension has the greatest impact on whether or not the ICC will ultimately be successful. Even if you have the best technology and well-defined processes that are aligned with the organization's needs, the ICC will not be successful if it is staffed with weak resources. On the other hand, if the ICC has strong technical and subject-matter expertise and strong leadership, it can overcome many technological shortcomings and process deficiencies. In short, if there is only one thing you do right, make sure you build a strong ICC team.

As you read through the following sections that describe each of the five ICC organizational models, keep in mind that they build on each other. For example, the evangelist activities described in the best-practices ICC are also critical to the other four ICC models.

5.2.1 Best-Practices ICC

The people who lead this effort are typically those in the organization who have solid integration experience and the passion to evangelize it. The primary focus in this ICC model is to identify practices that are working well (both inside the organization and externally) and promote them as broadly as possible. The two key roles are the knowledge coordinator and the training coordinator. Generally, one of the team members will also act as the ICC manager; alternatively, the manager of the group may have other IT responsibilities in addition to the ICC.

Below are the responsibilities of these two coordinators:

- **Knowledge coordinator**—Develops and maintains mapping patterns, reusable templates, and best-practices documents, usually stored in a central location and readily available to anyone in the enterprise.

- **Training coordinator**—Coordinates vendor-offered or internally sponsored training in specific integration technology products. Also prepares and delivers events such as seminars or internal presentations to various teams.

The size of this team may range from one person to a handful. But don't let the small size fool you; this team has the potential to have a big impact on the organization. If chosen well, the handful of core staff will form a much larger virtual team by enlisting evangelists from various functions across the enterprise. The virtual team can include architects, project managers, testing staff, developers, and others from diverse project teams.

5.2.2 Standard-Services ICC

The people within a standard-services ICC typically come from different development teams and may move from one team to another. However, at its core is a group of best-practices leaders. The number of staff may still be relatively small and some people may have more than one role. The most likely roles include the following, in addition to the best-practices roles:

- **Technology leader**—Responsible for vendor selection, management, and standards governance. This person should have very deep integration technology expertise and broad integration experience.

- **Metadata administrator**—Creates standards for capturing and maintaining metadata. The metadata repositories themselves will likely be maintained by various groups around the enterprise in a federated model, so the focus in this model is to define and enforce federated metadata standards and processes to sustain them.

- **Vendor manager**—Leads the efforts to select integration products and participates in the selection of vendors for the servers, storage, and network facilities needed for integration efforts. Handles vendor relationships on an ongoing basis, including maintaining awareness of trends, supporting contract negotiations, and escalating service and support issues.

- **ICC director**—Ensures that the ICC is in alignment with the IT strategy and anticipates business requirements. Manages the ICC staff, prepares business cases for integration investment initiatives, and is responsible for the annual budgets.

- **Standards analyst**—Actively monitors and promotes industry standards and adapts relevant ones to the needs of the enterprise. Defines, documents, and communicates internal enterprise standards. May also act as the company's official representative to external standards organizations, and may propose or influence the development of new industry standards.

5.2.3 Shared-Services ICC

The shared-services ICC has all the roles of the previous two models plus potentially eight additional roles. More significantly, the shared-services model may have a large number of staff who are organized as a COE; that is, they are available for short-term or long-term assignments to various project teams, but their permanent home is the ICC.

The additional roles within a shared-services ICC include:

- **Integration business analyst**—Facilitates solutions to complex, cross-functional business challenges; evaluates the applicability of technologies, including commercial ERP software; models business processes; and documents business rules concerning process and data integrations.

- **Change control coordinator**—Manages the migration to production of shared objects that may impact multiple project teams, determines impacts of changing one system in an end-to-end business process, and facilitates a common release schedule when multiple system changes need to be synchronized.

- **Data integration architect**—Provides project-level architecture review as part of the design process for data integration projects, develops and maintains the enterprise integration data model, supports complex data analysis and mapping activities, and enforces enterprise data standards.

- **Integration developer**—Reviews design specifications in detail to ensure conformance to standards and identify any issues upfront, performs detailed data analysis activities, develops data transformation mappings, and optimizes performance of integration system elements.

- **Product specialist**—Sets up and activates new software or hardware as it becomes part of the deployed architecture supporting the ICC, performs routine maintenance such as applying patches or version updates, and provides expert product support for incident or problem resolution.

- **Project manager**—Supplies full-time management resources experienced in data integration to ensure project success. Is adept at managing dependencies between teams, identifying cross-system risks, resolving issues that cut across application areas, planning complex release schedules, and enforcing conformance to an integration methodology.

- **Quality assurance manager**—Develops QA standards and practices for integration testing, furnishes data validation on integration load tasks, supports string testing (a "unit" test for integration elements) activities in support of integration development, and leads the execution of end-to-end integration testing.

- **Technical architect**—Develops and maintains the layout and details of the software configurations and physical hardware used to support the ICC, including tools for the ICC operations (for example, monitoring, element management, metadata repository, and scanning tools) or for the middleware systems (for example, message brokers, Web service application servers, and ETL hubs).

5.2.4 Central-Services ICC

The central-services ICC includes only four additional roles over those that are common to the shared-services ICC. But what is more significant is the scope of responsibility and how the team is organized. Under this model, the ICC will have a number of formally defined service-level agreements (SLAs) to support internal customers and full life-cycle responsibility for middleware systems, including ongoing support.

The ICC director and other roles previously defined are also present in the central-services model, but they may have a much broader set of responsibilities. For example, the ICC director is now responsible for SLA management, and a number of other roles shift from being "advisory" or "supporting" roles to direct accountability roles. The central-services model typically includes these additional roles:

- **Production operator**—Provides daily control and monitoring of integration jobs, responds to monitoring alerts, facilitates resolution of production incidents, reviews and approves changes to production configuration items, and performs routine maintenance activities (for example, backing up databases, purging log files, and cleaning up dead letter queues).

- **Repository administrator**—Ensures leverage and reuse of development assets, monitors repository activities, resolves data quality issues, and requests routine or custom reports.

- **Security administrator**—Provides access to the tools and technology needed to complete data integration development and overall data security, maintains middleware-access control lists, supports the deployment of new security objects, and handles configuration of middleware security.

- **Engagement manager**—Maintains the relationship with the internal customers of the ICC. Acts as the primary point of contact for all new work requests, supplies estimates or quotes to customers, and creates statements of work (or engagement contracts).

The central-services ICC may also operate as the equivalent of a fixed-price subcontractor to project teams for any and all interface development. In its most extreme form, the central-services ICC may be totally outsourced, a separate legal entity with contractually defined SLAs.

Although it may seem counterintuitive at first to outsource the integration function, if an enterprise's goals are efficiency and cost reduction, the quickest way to achieve them may be to treat the integration as a shared utility (as with the data network) and standardize it rapidly by outsourcing the function to a third-party organization.

5.2.5 Self-Service ICC

The self-service ICC has no new roles that haven't already been defined. However, the roles may be distributed back among the client organizations, in a virtualized model. The roles that are retained in this model focus primarily on administration roles related to operation of the middleware systems, coordination roles, governance of standards, and technical and management activities needed to deal with exceptions to normal operating procedures.

5.3 Organizing the ICC

There are as many ways to structure an ICC team as there are companies that have one. Factors driving the structure include the ICC model you select, the scope of responsibilities, the geographic distribution of the team, the strengths of the various team members, and the corporate culture, to name a few. If the team is relatively small, such as 5 to 10 members, you may not need any structure at all and simply have the entire staff report directly to the ICC director. If the team is very large, such as more than 100, you may need a more complex structure and a hierarchy of managers. Figure 5-2 shows a typical structure for a medium-size shared-services or central-services ICC.

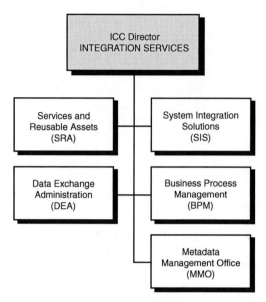

Figure 5-2. ICC Organizational Structure

What should you call your ICC and what should you put on the business cards of the staff? Whatever you want! The above chart is simply one example. The SRA team develops and maintains the enterprise shared code base, the Web services, and the enterprise service bus infrastructure. The SIS team handles all the message-based integrations between systems and supports portal technologies and data integration technologies. The DEA team resembles a DBA function but is in charge of all the middleware systems, including capacity management, availability management, incident management, change management, and the other ITIL processes. The BPM team supports the business team and functional teams with process analysis, modeling, deployment, and management. The MMO team develops all the metadata standards and maintains a federated repository of integration metadata, business data and process metadata, and IT infrastructure metadata.

We have also seen some creative job titles over the years, such as integration evangelist, business alignment manager, chief integration architect, and business process owner. You should use whatever title helps to communicate the role; it should have little to do with the job or salary level (although some organizations have strict rules about this—so don't fight it if you're in one of those companies).

One question we often hear is, "How many staff should be in the ICC?" Although there is no absolute answer to this question (it could be anywhere from one person to hundreds of people), there is a theoretical maximum size to the group. Various industry studies have pegged the cost of integration at 30 to 70 percent of the total cost of a typical large project, so one could argue that the largest size of a full-function central-services group would also be in this same range (say 50 percent on average). But since one of our arguments is that an ICC is more than twice as efficient as traditional silo integration, then we might peg the maximum size of a mature ICC at 25 percent of the total IT staff. But this is just theory. In practice, the largest ICC we have come across consists of around 180 staff, which represents 15 percent of the total IT organization.

5.4 Change Leadership Is Critical

A common theme throughout this book is that a successful ICC implementation is also a successful change management initiative. The challenges of changing an organization from one in which integration is a collaboration between two project silos to one in which integration is a common infrastructure based on strict standards and shared by everyone are substantial.

The relatively easy issues to overcome relate to rolling out new processes and having them be understood and accepted, new technology stability and performance issues, dealing with offshore and outsourcing demands, and finding competent staff. As tough as some of these issues might be, the solutions to them are relatively straightforward. The difficult challenges that you may run up against include:

- The "not invented here" syndrome and other similar "philosophies"

- Project funding by fine-grained business units that lack the money for and aren't motivated to solve the "big picture"

- Tactical short-term investment emphasis that doesn't appear to leave any room for strategic infrastructure investments

- Concessions and trade-offs required by functional teams to optimize the enterprise

- Autonomous operating groups in different locations that simply will not listen to or accept guidance from a central group

- Fear of change and vested interests in the status quo that come across as having no compelling reason to change

The term "challenges" might be too polite when referring to the preceding list; these seem a lot more like immovable barriers. As insurmountable as these hurdles seem, they are not unique to an ICC implementation and have been conquered in the past. Although there is no simple "silver bullet" solution, a number of key concepts have been proven over and over to be effective. All of them require a common ingredient: leadership. We could write a whole book about the topic of leadership (there are already thousands of books on the topic), but we will contain the discussion here to nine key ideas that are particularly relevant to ICCs.

5.4.1 Think Strategically, Act Tactically

The idea is to have a clear vision of the future, but to get there one step at a time. If you are fortunate enough to have an environment that allows you to secure lots of resources and have extensive executive support to invest in the strategy, that's great. But it's also very unusual. More commonly you will need to set your vision three to five years in the future and be patient enough to build the shared infrastructure in small increments, one project at a time.

Keep in mind the second law of integration (Section 2.3.2): *There is no end state.* In other words, in an integrated environment, something is always changing. For example, if you miss a window of opportunity to establish your new SOA standards on the latest approved ERP project, don't worry. Another project will come along. If you are in it for the long run, individual projects, even big ones, are just blips on the radar screen.

5.4.2 Gain Credibility Through Delivery

For others in the enterprise to see you as a leader, you need their trust and respect. Clearly, this means being open, honest, and trustworthy. But there is another dimension of trust: Do people trust that you will actually get the job done? This is probably the most important aspect of trust when you are trying to change a culture from "I want to do it my way" to "I will give up control to you because I believe you will do a good job, maybe even better than I could."

In the final analysis, having credibility comes down to your ability to execute: to organize your work, set suitable priorities, assign the appropriate resources to the task, and maintain good communications with your customers. Above all, keep your promises.

5.4.3 Grow Incrementally, Organically

A word of advice on growing the size of the ICC: Don't set out with an objective to grow a large team or have any specific target in mind for the number of staff. If focus centers on the size of the ICC team, it may appear to be a power grab and will cause people to become defensive. Rather, select a set of integration services that will be highly valued by the organization, staff it with good people, and be willing to accept new responsibilities as they come along. If you do this, and don't put up artificial barriers (such as budgets), you will find that the ICC grows naturally and organically to the "right" size.

5.4.4 Sidestep Resource Issues

In this global economy of outsourcing, offshoring, and contracting, you should always be able to find the resources to get a particular job done. If you want to create a reputation as a can-do ICC oriented to customer service, you should never have to say no to a service request because of lack of resources. (You may have another reason to say no, such as insufficient notice, very specific skill needs, or lack of conformance to standards, but that's another story.) For a shared-services or central-services ICC, you should always maintain a strong set of relationships with multiple external suppliers: middleware vendors, global consulting firms, and small local specialty firms. As long as you can maintain a core group of loyal permanent staff, you should be able to increase your workforce up to four or five times larger to handle peak workloads.

5.4.5 Choose Your Battles

Whenever you have the choice between a carrot or a stick approach, always use the carrot. You can, and should, carry a big stick in terms of having the support of the CIO and other executives for the ICC charter and for any mandated processes or standards, but use the power as infrequently as possible. Sometimes you may even need to make a concession on enforcing a standard that is clearly in the right from the ICC's perspective. You don't have to win every battle.

5.4.6 Take Out the Garbage

One way to help you choose your battles is to try this exercise. Write down your integration principles on a piece of paper. (If you don't know what they are off the top of your head, go back to Chapter 4). Then, one at a time, cross out the items that you would be willing to compromise on if pushed into a corner until you have only one left. Reserve your stick for that one principle.

We've already talked about growing incrementally and building credibility through delivery. Another dimension of those two ideas is to accept responsibility for work that no one else wants. If your security infrastructure is in a mess and your CIO is looking for someone to lead the single sign-on initiative that no one wants, put up your hand. If the internal auditors want someone to run around and inventory all holes in the firewall and any external FTP jobs, volunteer for that as well.

The interesting insight we have learned is that many of the jobs that no one really wants are those that don't serve a specific function and end up being ideal integration initiatives. Sometimes these also end up being really difficult challenges, which means they have a high probability of failure. But usually management will recognize these initiatives as difficult challenges, and if you at least tried your best to solve them, you won't end up with a black eye.

5.4.7 Leverage Knowledge

A well-known truism states that "knowledge is power." In an ICC, you are ideally positioned to talk with just about anyone in the IT organization—after all, you are in the middle. By asking a lot of questions and being a good listener, you can learn a lot about the organization that many project teams or other groups don't know. This knowledge can come in very handy in terms of which projects are getting approved and where you shouldn't spend your time, where next year's budget will land, which groups are hiring and which aren't, and so on.

The metadata repository is another source of knowledge (and power). If you have responsibility for all the documentation in the enterprise concerning data flows and dependencies between systems, you are ideally positioned to support (1) internal audit for some initiatives, (2) finance for asset inventory, (3) the disaster recovery team to build a continuity plan, and (4) business leaders when they want to outsource business processes. Each of these areas is an opportunity to provide value to an internal group that is likely to have some funding for an initiative at some point.

5.4.8 Refocus Innovation

Although there are major benefits to an ICC, there is also a downside: Standardization can stifle innovation. One could argue that innovation and variation are not essential for a shared infrastructure, yet there is always a tug-of-war between the forces of driving consistency and efficiency in the integration arena and staying ahead of the competition by innovating with new technologies. But rather than stopping innovation and discouraging individuals who are particularly good at implementing new ideas, we suggest steering those individuals to function-specific areas.

5.4.9 Take It Outside

Another aspect of leadership is active participation in the broader community—specifically, participation in standards bodies or professional organizations. The external activities can be useful for getting new ideas and insights and for polishing your own ideas though discussion and debate with others. In the end, these activities can make you stronger at an individual level, which can only help you lead inside your enterprise.

Chapter 6

ICC Capabilities

This chapter defines the processes that fall within the scope of ICC service delivery and the scope of responsibility the ICC group assumes in each of the five organizational models.

	Best Practices	Technology Services	Shared Services	Central Services	Self-Service
Integration Management					
Integration & Metadata Standards	○	●	●	●	●
Standards Governance	○	●	●	●	●
Integration Methodology	○	●	●	●	◉
Vendor Management		○	○	●	
Financial Planning & Management			○	○	
Technology Life-Cycle Management	○		○	●	
Program Management	○	○	◉	◉	
Enterprise Architecture	○	◉	◉	◉	
Service-Level Management		◉	○	○	
Information & Knowledge Services					
Metadata Management			○	●	
Application Portfolio Management			○	●	
Data Quality Management			○	●	
Business Intelligence			○	●	
Information Analytics			○	●	
Business Activity Monitoring			○	●	
Training & Education	●	●	●	●	●
Data Cleansing			○	●	

Legend

○   ICC provides support and/or resources for a decision or task in this functional area

◉   ICC has approved authority (right to veto) to stop decision/task and provides support

●   ICC is responsible for all aspects, provides support, and has veto rights

	Best Practices	Technology Services	Shared Services	Central Services	Self-Service
Solutions Delivery					
Shared Code Management	○	●	●	●	●
Shared Object Management	○	○	●	●	◉
Business Process Management			○	●	
Integration Project Management			○	●	
Integration Requirements Management			●	●	
Integration Architecture Review	○	○	●	●	◉
Integration Development			○	●	
Release Management			●	●	◉
Production Support					
Data Exchange Administration			◉	●	●
Security Management				○	
Change Management			○	◉	
Configuration Management			○	◉	
Incident Management				○	
Problem Management				○	
Service (Help) Desk Support				○	
Availability Management				○	
Capacity Management			○	◉	
Service Continuity Management			○	◉	

Legend

○ ICC provides support and/or resources for a decision or task in this functional area

◉ ICC has approved authority (right to veto) to stop decision/task and provides support

● ICC is responsible for all aspects, provides support, and has veto rights

Figure 6-1. ICC Capability Catalog

6.1 Integration Management

6.1.1 Integration and Metadata Standards

Integration and metadata standards are responsible for defining and communicating standards relating to processes, protocols, tools, and technology as it pertains to systems integration. Metadata in this context is more than "data about data"; it also includes data about systems, interfaces, servers, processes, security, and incidents. In many respects, the metadata standards are the foundation of an ERP for an IT system. This function works closely with standards governance to ensure compliance with the standards and reviewing environment changes in cooperation with configuration management.

Why they are important: A common approach is necessary to reduce the proliferation of point-to-point interfaces and integration complexity. There are more than 500 middleware vendors in the market, with an even larger number of product offerings. Many of the products are excellent, but at a practical level, no organization can support them all. The ICC must therefore choose the smallest subset of standards that is manageable and provides adequate functionality across the spectrum of needs.

Integration between applications is a shared infrastructure that can and should be optimized across the enterprise—even though for a given application the limited choices may not be ideal. Optimizing the whole system (the enterprise) implies that at least some subsystems will be suboptimized; trade-offs are a fact of life.

What it means: Simply defining standards is not sufficient. They must also be:

- Communicated through formal training initiatives

- Easily discoverable by new (permanent or temporary) staff

- Reviewed constantly and refreshed or updated regularly

- Applicable to all life-cycle phases, from development through production operations

- Enforced through a governance process

References: Integration Consortium, MDA, Object Management Group

6.1.2 Standards Governance

Standards governance is responsible for ensuring conformance to defined standards. It works most closely with enterprise architecture, program management, and change management to build in review and approval processes. Common checkpoints for standards may include approval of a project budget, completion of design or other project milestones, and migration to production.

Why it's important: Simply defining standards without adequate management controls is ineffective in many situations because conformance to standards often means making significant trade-offs among time, cost, and functionality. If left to individuals, the trade-offs will be made inconsistently. Controls are necessary to ensure that the standards are interpreted consistently and fairly.

What it means: Projects may choose between specifically defined options. If the defined options don't meet the need, a formal process must be followed to evaluate, select, and adopt a new enterprise standard to fill the need. In other words, a given project team can't just decide on their own.

If deviation from a standard is justified (for time to market or other reasons), the project should bear the cost of retrofitting to the standard and will not be considered "done" before doing so. The governance process must provide overall administration, including:

- Arranging and facilitating review meetings
- Obtaining formal management sign-offs for deviations from standards
- Providing standards compliance reports

References: Integration Consortium Integration Methodology

Integration methodology is responsible for defining the full life cycle of dependencies between application systems—from feasibility through design, build, and deploy to final retirement. In an ICC, integration means making multiple applications that were independently developed, may use incompatible technology, and remain independently managed work as one. The integration methodology is concerned with not just building quality solutions, but, more important, sustaining the solutions indefinitely in a production environment. The integration methodology processes are most closely aligned with the program management office, enterprise architecture, and production support.

Why it's important: Because the integration of applications has key differences in comparison to software engineering, it requires a specific methodology. Software development techniques have matured to a well-defined engineering discipline, but application integration at the enterprise level is still more of an art than a science in many organizations. For evidence of this, you need look no further than the unpredictability and high failure rate of large-scale integration efforts.

What it means: The scope of integration methodology is usually defined as "the enterprise," but we can apply this term at different levels. It usually refers to an entire corporate entity or government agency, but it could also refer to a subsidiary of a corporation or to a collection of entities operating as a supply chain within an industry. Regardless of the scope, the significant point is that integration methodology comes into play for multiapplication integration efforts, not for single applications. Some large applications are themselves complex enough that they use middleware technologies to facilitate integration of the application components, but don't confuse integrating components within an application with integration across applications.

References: Integration Consortium, Total Business Integration Methodology, Capability Maturity Model

6.1.3 Vendor Management

Vendor management involves maintaining relationships with suppliers of integration products and services. This activity includes negotiating terms and conditions, managing existing contracts, monitoring service levels of maintenance agreements, and staying abreast of new and emerging technologies. Vendor management is closely aligned with asset management and technology life-cycle management.

Why it's important: Many middleware technologies are highly distributed and may result in software assets deployed on hundreds or thousands of devices in virtually every location where the enterprise has computers. Central management of the components is necessary to ensure compliance with contract terms, such as regularly upgrading to supported versions of software, and to minimize costs by leveraging reusable assets efficiently.

What it means: From a vendor's perspective, an ICC can be both a positive and a negative. An organization that has a history of silo-driven investments may have a number of unused or underutilized assets spread throughout the enterprise. The early years of a newly established ICC could result in minimal new product acquisitions as the ICC consolidates fragmented systems to gain efficiencies and better utilize existing assets. On the other hand, some integration products offer little value to discrete project teams and offer a payback only when applied consistently across the enterprise. In this scenario, the ICC creates new opportunities for some vendor solutions.

References: Integration Consortium, ITscout

6.1.4 Financial Planning and Management

Financial planning and management processes are responsible for accounting for the costs and return on IT service investments and for any aspects of recovering costs from customers (charge back). They require good interfaces with service-level management and other processes to identify the true costs of service. These activities leverage the metadata repository (including information about the application portfolio, enterprise assets, project costs, and operations costs) to provide detailed information to the finance group.

Why they're important: Industry analysts and practitioners have often reported that integration costs range from 30 to 70 percent of total project cost. Furthermore, the total cost of ownership (TCO) is an increasingly important driver for many organizations and may be the key justification for establishing an ICC. Rapid development of silo solutions appears inexpensive initially, but the cost to maintain, operate, and change applications that have been tightly coupled with custom point-to-point interfaces eventually ends up costing many times the original development cost. CIOs and business executives are turning to ICCs to drive down integration costs, support TCO analysis, and leverage metadata to create greater transparency of charge backs to the business.

What it means: The metadata repository will grow into much more than just "data about data" once the finance group discovers it. There will quickly be pressure to link time reporting to applications for tracking maintenance and support costs, connecting projects to cost centers, and joining assets to business owners.

References: Integration Consortium

6.1.5 Technology Life-Cycle Management

Technology life-cycle management is the acquisition, deployment, management, and ultimate retirement of technologies that an organization uses. It involves: (1) staying abreast of market trends and evaluating emerging technologies through benchmarking, pilot initiatives, or proof-of-concept projects; (2) driving initiatives to upgrade technologies to newer versions when beneficial; and (3) obtaining the investments necessary to retire and eliminate legacy technologies when they no longer provide adequate value to the organization.

Why it's important: All phases of the life cycle are critical and all too often do not get sufficient attention in silo organizations. Silo organizations may select technologies because of their value to a single initiative, which may have a negative effect at the enterprise level. (For example, consider the high cost to integrate two proprietary databases into a common data warehouse.)

Maintaining current and supported versions of integration software is critical because, by definition, that software needs to interact with and support many other software packages, which also change over time. Although it may be feasible, and even desirable, to stop investing in maintenance of a legacy application that is supporting a stable and unchanging business process, never allow the interfaces between applications to become "legacy." Retirement is often the most difficult phase because it requires effort and money to eliminate cumbersome infrastructure, but often without a strong business payback justification. But in time, the legacy infrastructure slows change and using it is like swimming in molasses.

What it means: The challenge is in finding the balance between: (1) standardizing on proven technologies, which some people will regard as "legacy," and leveraging them consistently across the organization; and (2) innovating with new technologies. On one hand, an unchanging environment may be efficient in some respects, but it can soon stagnate and become a competitive disadvantage in comparison to newer technologies. On the other hand, a constantly changing and innovative environment will be chaotic and not achieve any significant measure of standardization within an enterprise.

References: Integration Consortium

6.1.6 Program Management

Program management as a discipline has been around since about 1991, in contrast with project management, which has a much longer history. Program management evolved during the 1990s as a management "layer" to coordinate the efforts of multiple independent business and technical projects teams toward a common goal. Program management ensures that all the teams work together in a coordinated manner to achieve a specific business goal. It does this through a number of activities, including (but not limited to):

- Documenting the common goals and ensuring that they are understood by all teams
- Developing and maintaining an integrated "big picture" of the solution
- Managing dependencies (something like contracts) between teams
- Identifying cross-team risks and developing proactive contingency plans
- Resolving or escalating interteam issues that could derail the program
- Conducting formal reviews and audits to retain a view of the "forest" as well as the "trees"
- Maintaining a realistic work plan and managing within a budget
- Engaging users (stakeholders) throughout the program's life cycle
- Ensuring a solid strategy for testing integration

The program management function works closely with portfolio management, release management, integration methodology, and financial management to accomplish the program's objectives.

Why it's important: Most large organizations will have dozens or even hundreds of projects in progress at any given time that will have some impact on changing the current IT infrastructure. Grouping the projects into programs and adding a layer of management to coordinate them is an effective way to maximize value to the organization. The bottom line: Do not undertake any large-scale program without a formal and disciplined approach to managing all its complexities.

What it means: Many organizations have a competency center for program management that's often called the enterprise program management office (EPMO). If so, it will be easier to establish and build an ICC because there is a clear group to work with; the ICC drives the integration practices across the enterprise, while the EPMO drives the program practices. If there is no EPMO or equivalent group, then the ICC will, by necessity, need to perform many of the key activities listed above.

Program management is increasingly called "portfolio management." Be aware that portfolio management is an overloaded term and may refer to either the enterprise IT operations as a whole (especially application portfolio management), or just the transformation initiatives (new spending) within it.

References: Integration Consortium, PMI, PMBOK

6.1.7 Enterprise Architecture

Enterprise architecture (EA) refers to the manner in which the operations, systems, and technology components of a business are organized and integrated. It defines many of the standards and structures of these components and is a critical aspect of allowing capabilities and their supporting applications to develop independently while all work together as part of an end-to-end solution. An EA consists of several component architectures, which often go by different names. Some of the common ones are:

- Business/functional architecture
- Data/information architecture
- Application/systems architecture
- Infrastructure/technology architecture
- Operations and execution architectures

An EA's core functions include these:

- Establish guiding principles for each of the architectural domains.

- Develop and maintain a reference model for each domain that defines terms, hierarchies, structures, and interrelationships in a generic framework.

- Document the current state of the baseline architecture using reference model standards.

- Create target architectures, which describe a desired future state in each domain.

- Develop a migration road map for the rationalization of the baseline architecture and establish steps to achieve the target architecture.

- Implement and oversee architecture methods and best practices across all architecture domains.

- Ensure widespread comprehension and use of architecture methods.

- Oversee and exercise governance of programs to guarantee compliance with target architectures and resolution of any related issues.

- Drive industry standards across all architecture domains.

Why it's important: The primary reason for developing an enterprise architecture is to support the business. An EA furnishes the fundamental technology and process structure for an IT strategy. This strategy in turn makes IT a responsive asset for a successful modern business strategy. An enterprise architecture provides a strategic context for the evolution of the IT systems in response to the constantly changing needs of the business environment.

What it means: There is no universal standard enterprise architecture, so each enterprise must create one. Fortunately, there are well-defined methods for creating an enterprise architecture. One of the best known is The Open Group Architecture Framework (TOGAF). If an organization has an established EA practice, it should be closely aligned with the ICC; ideally, both these functional groups could be under the same management structure. If there is no formal EA practice, then the ICC will need to perform many of the key activities listed above.

References: TOGAF

6.1.8 Service-Level Management

Service-level management (SLM) is responsible for ensuring that service-level agreements (SLAs) and their supporting underpinning contract obligations are met, and for keeping any adverse impact on service quality to a minimum. The process involves assessing the impact of changes on service quality and SLAs, both when changes are proposed and after they have been implemented. Some of the most important targets set in the SLAs will relate to service availability and thus require incident resolution within agreed periods.

Why it's important: The primary reason for service-level management is to handle expectations of business users (customers) of the IT operations. It is based on the principles that the IT function should: (1) explicitly categorize and describe the services it provides; (2) gain agreement with the business on the "level" of service that is needed and for which it is prepared to pay; and (3) manage the services to ensure that the expectations are met or exceeded.

What it means: Business users view IT delivery as a service—for example, email—which invariably consists of many hardware and software components that are part of a shared infrastructure. One component may play a role in many different services, which reinforces the importance of how effectively they are integrated. If an organization has an SLM practice, the ICC will need to work very closely with that function because many of the service levels will be achievable only through an effective integration infrastructure.

References: Integration Consortium, ITIL

6.2 Information and Knowledge Services

6.2.1 Metadata Management

Metadata management is responsible for maintaining information about IT people, processes, and technology. The term "metadata" is commonly understood as "data about data," but it has always included data about systems as well. Recently, the term has been expanding and evolving into new domains and ultimately includes the information for the enterprise IT function as a whole. The scope of metadata management may include information about application systems, components, interfaces, processes, events, databases, data elements, projects, documents, individuals, organizational units, devices, and incidents, to name a few topics. A mature metadata management practice is concerned with the dependencies between these components as well as the definitions of the components and how they are implemented.

Why it's important: The modern IT environment in a large organization: (1) is much too complex for any one person to understand; (2) has many elements with multiple relationships with other elements; (3) is constantly changing; and (4) needs to be managed from multiple perspectives—for example, financial, legal compliance, organizational, technical, and business unit. A "hairball" is a useful metaphor for describing this complexity. Traditional forms of documenting and analyzing the environment are ineffective. Metadata management is all about the technology needed to maintain a rich description of the business environment in a repository and the processes to support the information and keep it current.

What it means: One area not well addressed by any standards or notations is precisely documenting integration among distributed application systems. The heterogeneity of the typical IT environment is one of the challenges of integration. It encompasses a wide variety of technologies: messaging, FTP, database middleware, application servers, message brokers, and more. Integration metadata is concerned with end-to-end semantics. It explores how, given system A and system B, data moves between them and business processes are supported. Integration metadata is more difficult than the well-established discipline of "data about data" because definitions of "systems" and "processes" are themselves abstract logical concepts. In other words, the problem is not one that can be solved simply through an analytical process; it requires an agreement process.

References: MDA, OMG, ERP4IT

6.2.2 Application Portfolio Management

Application portfolio management (APM) is responsible for developing and maintaining the list of application systems in the enterprise, as well as information about the systems. APM works closely with metadata management, because applications are one of the key entities that an organization is concerned about managing and tracking. APM is also very closely aligned with program management, financial management, and enterprise architecture.

Why it's important: This information is critical to managing the interconnections in the environment to avoid duplication of integration efforts and to know when particular integration feeds are no longer needed. Understanding interdependencies between systems is critical for maintaining stable operations by knowing how a change to one system may affect another, and for optimizing end-to-end business processes.

What it means: For an ICC to effectively have responsibility for integrating systems, it must first define what a system is. The precise definition of a "system" is a logical concept, which means that it is subject to interpretation. As a general rule, a system has a single business owner, a single IT manager, and a single IT architect. The net effect is that it is possible to create new systems or collapse multiple systems into one simply by making an organizational change. The APM process is therefore not a one-time effort to define the applications, but rather an ongoing process that considers organizational and people issues as well as technology, architecture, and program initiatives. As a process, it will require clear stakeholders and actors. Establishing that some group of functionality will be called a "system" is a significant enterprise decision, analogous to establishing a new entry in the financial chart of accounts.

References: ERP4IT

6.2.3 Data Quality Management

Data quality management is an often-misunderstood concept. It is the process of ensuring that data remains consistent, accurate, and fit for its intended purpose. Maintaining data quality is a process that spans the entire life cycle, from data entry through its valuable life in a transactional system to its analytic value in a decision support system.

Why it's important: Two constituents need consistent and accurate data to operate efficiently. Those constituents are the transactional systems and the business users. Without a process for maintaining high-quality data in the transactional systems, the order-entry system may contain a record that conflicts with the invoice system, the shipping system, and the accounts receivable system. Which system contains the right information and how many customers have churned because they were billed for an item that was never shipped?

What it means: Maintaining consistent, accurate data across systems is often the responsibility of a data steward. Good data stewardship involves understanding not only the technical considerations for providing systems with consistent, accurate data, but also the business considerations, such as how the data will be consumed by business users, and the fitness of the data for its intended application.

References: Integration Consortium (IC), The Data Management Association (DAMA), Total Data Quality Management program (TDQM)—see http://web.mit.edu/tdqm/ www/index.shtml Data Warehousing and Business Intelligence

Data warehousing and business intelligence (BI) provide reports and dashboards on operational aspects of the business. Typically these practices involve integrating data from a variety of operational sources into a data mart or a data warehouse and querying statistics from the normalized, integrated data. Business users rely on the BI function to provide the information necessary to make informed decisions.

Why they're important: BI enables business users to obtain key performance indicators and analysis (for example, for a particular business process to determine what happened, why something happened, and what could or will happen) from their operational applications and decision support processes. This information allows them to gain a more accurate and effective picture of the business and its environment. As a result, BI tools enable an organization to better manage its business and realize increased value from its IT investments in its operational applications.

What it means: The data warehouse is a system unto itself. Therefore, an ICC needs to consider it as such and maintain it properly. Often the responsibilities for integrating data into the data warehouse belong to a different person from whoever produces the reports and troubleshoots the query and reporting tool. It is critical to maintain close communication between those responsible for the data and those responsible for the reporting. These are two sides of a single coin and require collaboration to ensure that the data is organized in a manner that will produce accurate query results and consistent metrics.

References: Integration Consortium, Mr. Bill Inmon, Dr. Ralph Kimball, TDWI

6.2.4 Business Activity Monitoring

Business activity monitoring (BAM) is responsible for the real-time monitoring of business metrics and for issuing alerts when problems or opportunities arise. Ideally, BAM should allow process owners to respond in real time, rather than after the fact, to events that impact the business. BAM processes involve collecting many events, correlating related events, applying business rules or policies to determine if the events are within normal operating boundaries, and taking action when events move outside of defined limits.

Why it's important: The demand for BAM in enterprises is growing, triggered by the faster pace of business, which encourages speedy detection of problems and opportunities. New regulations, such as the Sarbanes-Oxley Act, the U.S. Health Insurance Portability and Accountability Act, and the Patriot Act, bring up the issue of monitoring compliance, which BAM can address.

What it means: BAM is rarely associated with a single business application or IT function, and it is often related to business processes that cut across organizational and functional boundaries. For this reason, the ICC group often ends up responsible for it. BAM is both technology and process, and its focus is real-time intervention and prevention based on events and alerts, using dashboard indicators as the primary mechanism for presenting key metrics and their measures to the business.

References: Integration Consortium, Adaptive Business Process Management

6.2.5 Training and Education

Training and education are responsible for communicating the ICC practices and standards and for driving the organizational change activities throughout the enterprise. Methods to accomplish these activities may range from "evangelism" (for example, creating awareness of integration concepts, building confidence in the ICC model, and fostering a willingness to change) to formal training programs (for example, training guidebooks, self-paced Web-enabled learning resources, lunch-box seminars, and lecture-style classroom sessions).

Why it's important: ICCs are a new way of operating in most organizations. The traditional operating model has been silo project teams strongly aligned with functional business areas, both of which typically have a lot of latitude in making design decisions and selecting technologies. Each of the five ICC approaches needs to create a paradigm shift in thinking and behavior if it is to be effective. Training and eduction programs are essential elements of driving changes in behavior throughout the organization.

What it means: Of all the ICC process areas, training and education are the most fundamental processes for ensuring that the ICC is accepted and adopted across the enterprise. They make up the only process area that the ICC is responsible for regardless of which organizational model is selected. In other words, training and education are essential prerequisites for achieving the benefits from an ICC.

References: Integration Consortium

6.3 Solutions Delivery Support

6.3.1 Shared Code Management (Frameworks)

Shared code management is responsible for providing enterprise-class software components that can be easily reused for any in-house application development project. These components, usually called "frameworks," integrate a blend of best-of-breed third-party components and custom features that implement standard IT functions in the enterprise to furnish development teams with tools needed to create robust and reliable applications rapidly. Most ICCs will develop and maintain a framework in .NET and/or Java. The framework also provides process guidelines on standards and best practices, complete with checkpoints at critical phases to ensure the smooth progression of projects through their complete life cycle.

Why it's important: In a competitive business climate, it is too expensive to develop applications without first having a structure in place. It's like trying to build a house without first installing the framework. Faced with business demands for efficiency and lower costs, enterprise IT departments need solid, repeatable, and proven infrastructures to facilitate fast development time. With the proper framework, a development project can immediately concentrate on getting the product out instead of getting stuck trying to ramp up. Using a framework enables the ICC to:

- Jump-start projects by providing out-of-the-box solutions for functions commonly needed across multiple application development efforts.

- Facilitate the deployment and monitoring of applications—key elements of project planning that development teams often ignore.

- Provide access to well-tested components that accommodate a wide spectrum of application functional needs.

- Prevent application teams from rolling their own solutions to address these needs so that the enterprise environment is not cluttered with a variety of redundant products.

- Enable development teams to focus completely on the needs of the business they serve, rather than on the complexities of the application's infrastructure.

What it means: Even when organizations have a strong "buy versus build" principle, it is rare for any IT group to not do any internal development. In fact, if an organization were to buy 100 percent of its application systems from vendors, it would still need to integrate those applications and link them to customers and external partners, which means that the ICC would drive 100 percent of the development. For this reason, the ICC must retain responsibility for shared code management. The reuse challenge has synergies with metadata management.

References: Integration Consortium

6.3.2 Shared-Services Management (Web Services)

Shared-services management is responsible for the development, maintenance, and support of interfaces to common business functions. It is also often referred to as service oriented architecture, enterprise service bus, or Web services. Web services standards will be evolving very rapidly. Web services are the basis for the integration solutions that provide the request/reply integration pattern, although it is possible to use them for other patterns. The standards that apply to Web services supply consistent building and management of interfaces to common business functions.

Why it's important: The primary reasons for shared-services management are to: (1) reduce costs by minimizing the need to copy and maintain replicated databases; (2) enable efficient business processes by furnishing access to data in the system of record in real time; (3) simplify the infrastructure by implementing only one set of standards to support the request/reply integration pattern; and (4) reduce the time to build new applications by assembling common functions that already exist in the enterprise into a new composite application.

What it means: Although the technology of Web services is generally well understood, it can be confusing, since more than 50 established and emerging standards exist. The bigger challenge is to gain alignment with the business. Creating an "enterprise" service can be just as challenging as creating an optimized cross-functional business process. It is necessary to identify a business owner for the enterprise services, understand what internal "market" exists for the service (that is, who will use it), establish a campaign to promote the service to other business functions, maintain the service, and ultimately retire the service when it is no longer needed. In short, shared-services management is more than a technical activity; it requires a collaborative working relationship with a business partner.

Again, managing the reuse challenge for dozens or hundreds of Web services can follow the metadata management platform.

References: Web Services

6.3.3 Business Process Management

Business process management (BPM) is responsible for automating business processes with the emphasis on the ability to monitor and manage processes in real time, including human-to-human, system-to-system, and system-to-human processes. It is concerned with managing cross-functional processes effectively. At the business level, BPM is the management of explicit processes from beginning to end.

Why it's important: There are many dimensions to the integration challenge, including data, systems, processes, platform, operations, business unit, and geography. Although all dimensions are critical, we need to choose one as the anchor point to begin analyzing problems, modeling solutions, and driving changes. The key benefit from integration is not simply creation of a collection of interfaces, but provision of service to all business operations and ultimately the entire supply chain. In this regard, the business processes dominate and drive value to the enterprise.

What it means: Traditional methodologies anchor requirements around application functions and data, rather than around enterprise processes. This approach is inadequate for enterprise integration. We need a standard enterprisewide methodology for describing and modeling end-to-end business processes with particular emphasis on those that are cross-functional.

Interfaces need to be associated with the business processes they support. In production, the failure of a given integration component should be analyzed from the standpoint of the business processes it would impact. This means that capturing the metadata associated with the business process and associated data is critical. It is also necessary to clearly identify owners within the business who have management responsibility for end-to-end processes.

A number of enterprise issues need to be considered when discussing BPM. For BPM to be most effective, it should be integrated with business process analysis, business activity monitoring, a wide range of IS execution environments, and infrastructure monitoring tools. Minimally, it must be able to model business processes, enable those processes from an IS perspective, and provide a business view into executing the processes.

References: Integration Consortium, Adaptive Business Process Management

6.3.4 Integration Project Management

Integration project management is responsible for all the integration activities associated with a given project or program. Integration project management activities include defining the integration scope, sizing and costing the integration effort, preparing detailed project plans, coordinating the integration tasks and deliverables, facilitating communications across the various systems teams, managing integration risks and issues, and ensuring a smooth hand-off to production support teams. Integration project management works closely with program management, enterprise architecture, integration methodology, and all the teams within solutions delivery.

Why it's important: In the shared-services or central-services ICC model, interfaces are treated as shared infrastructure rather than as components of the applications being integrated. As such, every integration that impacts the shared infrastructure must be carefully managed to ensure that no unintended consequences result from the new integration.

What it means: The integration project management role in an ICC can be very challenging at times because it may require facilitation or negotiation skills to gain agreement on competing, and sometimes conflicting, activities. For example, despite the loose coupling principles and the use of isolation technologies such as XML, a new version of a payroll system may be so significant that it requires a change to the financial system. The owner of the financial system may not be prepared to make the change or may not be able to do it in the time frame necessary for the payroll system deployment. This sensitive matter may be difficult to gain agreement on, especially in situations with tight budget or resource constraints or conflicting priorities in the two different business units. You need a strong manager in this role who has senior management support.

References: PMI, PMBOK, Integration Consortium

6.3.5 Integration Requirements Management

Integration requirements management maintains the enterprise integration model (sometimes called the "canonical model") and documents the data mappings and transformations between systems as well as other technical integration requirements—for example, performance, security, confidentiality, monitoring, event notification, and platform-specific needs. This function works closely with business process management, metadata management, shared object management, integration development, and data exchange administration to perform activities, including impact assessment of proposed changes, business analysis for data transformations, and transformation modeling.

Why it's important: Each system, regardless of how well coordinated the development is between them, will have some differences in the format, structure, and business rules associated with the application data. This situation shows why you need an enterprise canonical (or standard) data definition. Applications may be more loosely coupled if each system's data is translated into a common format before being handed off to another system. This common format simplifies the integration environment and promotes data reuse.

What it means: The number of interfaces and the correspondingly even larger number of data attributes involved in integrations between systems, plus the constantly changing nature of a typical IT environment, mean that requirements cannot be maintained in Microsoft Word documents or spreadsheets. Integration requirements need to be maintained in a well-structured searchable database with a formal data model. Furthermore, the analysts working in this group must be familiar with industry-standard modeling conventions, such as Unified Modeling Language (UML).

References: Integration Consortium

6.3.6 Integration Architecture Review

Integration architecture review is responsible for applying the relevant enterprise standards in each initiative involving integration between two or more systems. This function works closely with standards governance, enterprise architecture, and integration development to help interpret the technology decision tree, resolve conflicts between standards or principles, and initiate exceptions when deviation from standards is warranted. (Note: Obtaining management approval of any deviation is the responsibility of standards governance.)

Why it's important: Publishing integration principles and standards, and communicating them across the organization, is not sufficient to ensure that the standards are followed because:

- Standards may sometimes have overlapping specifications or make conflicting statements.

- Standards are constantly evolving, and not everyone will be aware of the latest developments.

- Principles are necessarily high-level statements, and it may not be obvious how to apply them in a given situation.

- Different standards may be documented at various levels of detail.

For these reasons, it is necessary to interpret the standards in the context of a specific initiative, which is the role of an integration/architecture review board.

What it means: Architectural principles offer useful guidance to project teams, but each situation is unique and requires a judgment call on how to apply the guidelines. In most cases, different people will interpret the guidelines in the same way, but because they are high-level statements, different interpretations may be possible in certain situations.

References: Integration Consortium

6.3.7 Integration Development

Integration development handles the design, development, testing, and deployment of software and hardware elements needed for a given integration. Although the specific tools and software artifacts produced in an integration system may differ somewhat from an application system, the activities themselves associated with this function are traditional software and systems engineering activities.

Why it's important: The primary reason for this function is to ensure that interfaces are well engineered, reliable, and robust. There can be a great deal of value in having a central services group do the integration engineering because that group can apply the lessons learned from one integration to the next. In particular, the integration development team should constantly refactor interface software to include the capabilities of handling the nuances of different platforms and protocols.

What it means: Many organizations have a "buy versus build" principle, which means that the vast majority of the actual in-house development is, in fact, integration development. As a result of this trend, there is an increasing number of middleware open source initiatives that development teams can leverage, including OpenJMS, open adapter, and OpenLDAP.

References: Integration Consortium, CMM

6.3.8 Release Management

Release management is responsible for the definition, control, and implementation of "packaged releases" that may result from the need for new hardware, new versions of software, or coordinated functional changes across multiple applications. The procedures for achieving a secure, managed rollout should be closely integrated with those for enterprise architecture, change management, configuration management, and metadata management. Release procedures may also be an integral part of incident management and problem management, as well as being closely linked to the CMDB and metadata repository to maintain up-to-date records.

Why it's important: Although release management is important for controlling the changes in a given system, it takes on increased importance, and increased complexity, when multiple independently managed systems are involved. Over time, the institutional knowledge concerning dependencies between applications may become lost, which results in operational "surprises" as a result of a production change. The responsibility of release management is to maintain stable production operations by carefully controlling changes involving multiple systems. Release management performs the work authorized by change management and governed by configuration management.

What it means: Successfully compiling and deploying software in a consistent and predictable manner is often challenging because the environments are complex and the state-of-the-art tools are not well integrated, so they require a lot of manual attention. Typically, source code repository systems are used for storing versions of tracking source code. These systems allow a user to check software into and out of the system, track versions, maintain security, and monitor dependencies between code segments. When the code is ready to be compiled, the source code is checked out and submitted to a building engine for a compilation. The compiled code is stored in the definitive software library and is usually deployed into a testing environment before the release to the production environment, depending on the current status of the developed code. This deployment is typically accomplished by placing the compiled code in a staging directory used by a content deployment and replication engine. By placing the code in the correct location in the staging directory, the deployment and replication engine can determine the locations to which the compiled code should be deployed. In addition, uncompiled code data, such as content, off-the-shelf executables, and configuration objects, can also be stored in a source code repository and deployed by a content deployment and replication engine.

The metadata repository and the definitive software library or CMDB are increasingly essential resources in large organizations. They help to enable a systematic process for controlling releases of production changes in an efficient manner without depending solely on tacit knowledge that is kept only in the minds of enterprise staff.

References: Integration Consortium, ITIL

6.4 Production Support

6.4.1 Data Exchange Administration

Data exchange administration (DEA) is similar to database administration (DBA), except that the DEA's key responsibilities are ensuring that data is available for all production systems as required. This includes ongoing monitoring and maintenance to verify that the integration systems are functioning efficiently. The DEA works closely with all other production support functions and has the following responsibilities:

- Provide production support for interface incidents and problems

- Maintain operational standards and naming conventions for middleware infrastructure objects

- Define and monitor service-level agreements concerning data movement

- Maintain end-to-end data flow documentation in the metadata repository

- Approve changes to the production environment

- Administer the security of the middleware infrastructure and integration systems

Why it's important: Integration systems require an ongoing administration function just as application systems do. The DEA function is not only necessary to maintain stable operations, but it can also have a strong payback by doing performance optimization and server consolidation for organizations that previously operated in production silos.

What it means: Data exchange administration is a new role for most organizations, so there may be some organizational resistance to its acceptance. It is particularly important to link the DEA function with other production support teams and is most important in the central-services and self-service ICC models.

References: Integration Consortium

6.4.2 Security Management

Security management interfaces with IT service management processes where security issues are involved. Such issues relate to the confidentiality, integrity, and availability of data, as well as the security of hardware and software components, documentation, and procedures. For example, security management interfaces with service management to assess the impact of proposed changes on security, to raise requests for change in response to security problems, to ensure confidentiality and integrity of security data, and to maintain security when software is released into the live environment.

Why it's important: Security of middleware infrastructure has always been important, but the Sarbanes-Oxley Act has brought the need to the forefront for all U.S.-based organizations because of its requirements regarding the traceability of financial information. Other regulations in Europe, the United States, and other areas are placing increased emphasis on customer privacy and confidentiality. These regulations also increase the need to secure and carefully control access to information, not just as it resides in application databases, but also as the information moves around the organization.

What it means: The implications for middleware security are very significant. FTP may no longer be an acceptable file transfer method and may need to be replaced with SFTP (secure FTP); a central authentication service may need to control authorization for access to message queues; and the use of certificates and two-way authentication in Web services may place greater demands on metadata management to administer and track certificates, holes in the firewall, and external systems. The list could go on, but you get the idea.

References: IT Infrastructure Library, Integration Consortium

6.4.3 Change Management

Change management involves controlling changes to configuration items by approving and scheduling requested changes. The process depends on the accuracy of the configuration data to ensure that the full impact of making changes is known. There is a very close relationship among configuration management, release management, change management, and metadata management. SLAs document details of changes to ensure that users know the procedure for requesting changes and the projected target times for and impact of the implementation of changes. The service desk needs to know the details of changes. Even with comprehensive testing, there is an increased likelihood of difficulties occurring following change implementation, either because the change is not working as required or expected, or because of queries on the change in functionality. Members of the change advisory board (CAB) give expert advice to the change management team on the implementation of changes.

Why it's important: Complex production environments frequently consist of dozens or even hundreds of servers. These servers are often based on different operating platforms, such as UNIX, Linux, MVS, and Windows NT, each of which adds complexities and dependencies that need to be carefully considered. The systems that are deployed on these servers often consist of thousands of individual files and components with a complex web of dependencies among them. If just one small link in the chain is missing or broken, the entire system may crash. Furthermore, it is necessary to maintain multiple parallel environments—such as development, testing, training, and production—also in consistent states and to carefully propagate changes from one environment to the next in a controlled and safe manner. Change management is more than gatekeeping for the production environment. It is concerned with impact analysis and risk assessment, alignment with the release management plan, and review of the implementation of authorized changes to ensure that the requested changes were implemented as planned.

What it means: Unfortunately, few environments adequately integrate source code repositories, compilers, and deployment engines. As a result, the delivery of new software components and updates to the development testing and production environments is often inconsistent, error prone, and time consuming. It takes hours, sometimes even days, before a new working version of an application or an update can be deployed into a specified environment. And most challenging of all is when it becomes necessary to roll back the entire environment into the last working version when particular updates do not work. Because there is no adequate integration of the tools, the coordination of source code, building and deployment, and the handling of rollbacks are accomplished to a large degree manually. This manual effort is a test of patience, concentration, and precision. The slightest mistake can render an application or an entire site unusable until it is fixed.

References: Integration Consortium, ITIL

6.4.4 Configuration Management

Configuration management is an integral part of all other integration management and production support processes. With current, accurate, and comprehensive information about every component of the infrastructure, the management of change, in particular, is more effective and efficient. At a minimum, we recommend that a comprehensive configuration management system controls the logging and implementation of changes and that it helps in assessing the impact and risk of changes. All change requests should be entered in the configuration management database (CMDB) and the records updated as the change request progresses to implementation.

Why it's important: The importance of configuration management is strengthened by the high complexity in most IT environments and the weak versioning conventions for deployed software. Existing control systems focus on version control for source code only, but do not carefully maintain version information for the code and content deployed into an environment. As a result, tracking the components that exist in an environment can be difficult. Finally, there is no effective way to obtain a full component inventory from any environment. Without such an inventory, the integrity of the environments cannot be guaranteed and can only be accepted as is. This often results in unpredictable application behavior when components are moved among the development, testing, and production environments.

What it means: The CMDB is not necessarily a single data store and may be combined in certain cases with the metadata repository (MDR) because many off-the-shelf CMDB systems have a rather weak data model in comparison to the MDR. The intent of a configuration management system is to identify relationships between an item that is to be changed and any other components of the infrastructure, thus allowing the owners of these components to be involved in assessing the impact. Most CMDBs, however, are not designed to capture complex relationships and integration metadata among multiple configuration items, so you need to involve the MDR in this process as well. Whenever a change is made to the infrastructure and/or services, update associated CMDB and MDR records. Where possible, this is best accomplished with integrated tools that update records automatically as changes are made. Vendors of both types of products should be encouraged to drive toward convergence and industry standards.

References: IT Integration Library, ERP4IT

6.4.5 Incident Management

Incident management identifies events that are not part of the standard operation of a service and that impact (or may impact) the quality of that service. It also handles the processes to address the incident and return the service to defined levels. There should be a close interface among the incident management process and the problem management and change management processes as well as the function of the service desk. If not properly controlled, changes may introduce new incidents. A way of tracking back is necessary. Store incident records in the same CMDB as the problem and change records, or at least link them without the need for rekeying, and associate them with one or more configuration items. Incident priorities and escalation procedures need to be established as part of the service-level management process and documented in the SLAs.

Why it's important: Integration systems are often "invisible" to a business user—until they stop working. Although integration systems often move data between systems as part of a critical business process, users typically don't interact with the integration systems, so they may not be aware of them. Nonetheless, disruptions to integration data flows can bring a critical business process to a standstill, which makes the task of returning the system to defined services levels extremely critical.

What it means: An ICC in a central-services or self-service model requires staff coverage 24x7, with defined escalation levels. Even the ICC director needs to be prepared to assist with service recovery.

References: ITIL

6.4.6 Problem Management

Problem management is responsible for identifying known errors, defining work-arounds, and permanently resolving the underlying cause of one or more incidents. The problem management process requires the accurate and comprehensive recording of incidents to identify the cause of the incidents and trends effectively and efficiently. Problem management also needs to work closely with the capacity and availability management processes to identify these trends and instigate remedial action.

Why it's important: Individual production incidents on their own may not have a big impact, but a pattern of incidents may highlight a serious underlying problem that should be resolved. Separating problem management from incident management is important because it is generally not acceptable to add long delays in service recovery in the interest of root-cause analysis.

What it means: A pattern of incidents over a long time may indicate that the integration systems are not functioning properly or may be handling certain error conditions in a robust fashion. Furthermore, production support teams may become very efficient at responding to and resolving recurring incidents and may not be motivated (or lack time) to perform root-cause analysis. An effective program management function can have a big payback in terms of reducing support costs and production outages.

References: ITIL

6.4.7 Service (Help) Desk Support

The **service desk** (also called the help desk) is the single point of contact between service providers and users on a day-to-day basis. It is in the direct firing line of any impact on the SLAs and as such needs rapid information flows. Change management should ensure that the service desk is constantly kept aware of change activities. The service desk may be delegated to implement changes to resolve incidents within its sphere of authority. The scope of such changes should be predefined, and the change management function should be informed about all such changes.

Why it's important: The service desk is a focal point for reporting incidents and making service requests. As such, the service desk has an obligation to keep users informed of service events, actions, and opportunities that are likely to impact their ability to pursue their day-to-day activities.

What it means: Because the integration systems are often invisible to the end users, they will likely not be able to give a good problem description to the service desk. For example, a person is likely to describe a problem as, "The order management system is not working. All of today's purchase orders are not showing up," rather than, "None of today's POs were loaded into the order management system despite the fact that the PO system sent them." It is essential that the service desk staff have good training and good reference material on critical business processes that cut across several business systems so that they can ask the right questions.

References: ITIL

ICC Capabilities

6.4.8 Availability Management

Availability management deals with the design, implementation, measurement, and management of IT services to ensure that the stated business requirements for availability are consistently met. Availability management requires an understanding of the reasons why IT services fail and the time necessary to resume service. Incident management and problem management furnish key input to ensure that the appropriate corrective actions are in progress. Availability targets specified in SLAs are monitored and reported on as part of the availability management process. In addition, availability management supports the service-level management process in providing measurements and reporting to support service reviews.

Why it's important: In an integrated environment, availability of the end-to-end process impacts the availability of each component of the process. Availability management must maintain a perspective of the availability of enterprise business processes, and not just the components, because that is how end users will perceive the effectiveness of IT.

What it means: Even if an enterprise has a low level of maturity for its business process management—inconsistent processes without a well-defined hierarchy—every organization has cross-functional business processes that are critical to its operation. Some of the processes may be hard coded in batch jobs and may not be explicitly defined, but they exist nonetheless, which means that the ICC needs to understand them and maintain an eye toward end-to-end process availability.

References: Integration Consortium

6.4.9 Capacity Management

Capacity management ensures that adequate capacity is available at all times to meet business requirements. It involves far more than the performance of the system's components, individually or collectively. Capacity management also deals with resolving incidents and identifying problems for those difficulties relating to capacity issues.

Why it's important: The capacity demands on the integration infrastructure may not be visible to the functional application teams because many applications may share the same integration systems. The ICC must consolidate and aggregate the needs from all applications.

What it means: Integration capacity is not simply the sum of capacity needs of each application. A temporal dimension must be considered as well. Different applications will place different workload demands on the integration infrastructure at different times, so if we simply add up all the individual peaks, the integration system may be oversized and too expensive.

References: Integration Consortium, ITIL

6.4.10 Service Continuity Management

Service continuity management, also known as disaster recovery, is responsible for continuing to provide a predetermined and agreed level of IT services to support the minimum business requirements following an interruption to the business. Effective IT service continuity requires a balance of risk reduction measures, such as resilient systems and recovery options that include back-up facilities. Configuration management data facilitates this prevention and planning infrastructure. Business changes need to be assessed for their potential impact on the continuity plans, and the IT and business plans should be subject to change management procedures.

Why it's important: Simply recovering application systems without recovering their interfaces after a disruption may not be very effective. For example, if orders can't get from the order management system to the fulfillment system, then neither system will operate effectively. In any organization with robust integration systems, the integration systems themselves must be quickly recoverable.

What it means: The metadata repository (MDR) may be one of the most critical systems in the enterprise. A mature, well-established MDR contains much of the institutional knowledge about the rest of the IT systems and operations, so if it cannot be recovered after a business interruption, it could delay the recovery of all other systems and processes. It is therefore critical to recover the MDR first after an outage.

References: Integration Consortium, IT Integration Library

Chapter 7

ICC Technology

This chapter provides a reference definition of the technology areas that fall within the scope of ICC service delivery and the scope of responsibility the ICC group assumes in each of the five organizational models.

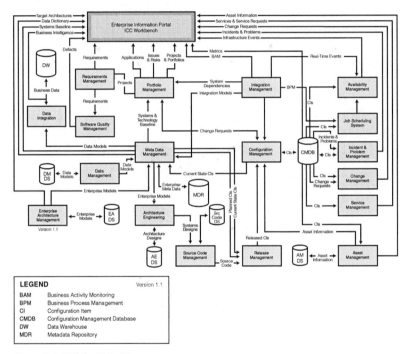

LEGEND   Version 1.1

BAM	Business Activity Monitoring
BPM	Business Process Management
CI	Configuration Item
CMDB	Configuration Management Database
DW	Data Warehouse
MDR	Metadata Repository

Figure 7-1. ERP for IT Architecture

Figure 7-1 starts by setting the scope of technologies that an ICC may need to deal with in an all-encompassing ICC. If all of these technologies were tightly integrated, built on a coherent data model, and implemented with tools that supported the IT processes, we could call it the ERP for the IT system. The reality, however, is that no such system exists. The typical large enterprise has a collection of best-of-breed systems that have incompatible data models and are manually synchronized.

The purpose of this book is not to solve the ERP for IT challenge (that is a huge topic on its own), but to provide a context for the ICC to focus on selected technologies that are most relevant to integration and a way to think about how to effectively integrate with the rest of the IT scope.

With all the industry buzzwords and rapid development of new technologies, the integration technology spectrum can be extremely confusing. Let's take a step back and look at the basics, starting with the simple model in Figure 7-2.

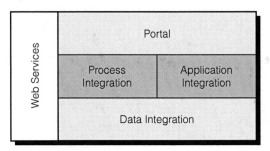

Figure 7-2. Integration Technologies

Every application has three layers: (1) user interface, (2) business rules or processing logic, and (3) data. Conceptually, this model hasn't changed in the past 20 years, but what has changed are the languages, protocols, standards, and sophistication of the tools to enable the logical separation of the layers. In any event, the basic idea of a three-tier application architecture is still valid today.

Each of the three layers has unique characteristics, which in turn drive a unique integration technology (see Figure 7-3). It is possible to mix and match some of the technologies, but first let's look at them separately.

Integrating at the user interface is sometimes called "integrating at the glass." The most common way to enable this integration is with portal technologies. An Internet Web browser is a form of portal technology.

The term "application integration" is usually applied to systems that are interacting with each other without the involvement of a human being. This occurs most commonly through an application programming interface (API) with message oriented architectures or with service oriented architectures. The technologies have changed over the years, but the architectural patterns have not: 20 years ago it was CICS; 10 years ago the prevailing technologies and standards were CORBA, COM, RPC, and FTP; today they are Web services and JMS. Of course, many of the legacy technologies are still in operation today. In fact, FTP remains one of the most commonly used protocols, even with new applications, because it is simple and widely supported.

Note that application integration may include both reading directly from the user interface layer or the data layer and writing directly to either of these layers. These practices are generally not considered ideal because they tend to tightly couple applications in ways that are hard to manage; however, they are valid techniques that sometimes are desirable (especially in the case of certain legacy environments that lack well-defined or supported APIs).

Integrating at the data layer generally requires data aggregation architectural patterns. Most commonly, it involves a data mart or a data warehouse, but this type of integration often occurs at the data layer in a variety of patterns. The core idea is that because an organization has many systems, each with its own data store, a consolidated view of the information is essential for producing decision support systems and for operational efficiencies related to the applications.

Figure 7-3 offers a more comprehensive list of integration technologies.

	Best Practices	Technology Services	Shared Services	Central Services	Self-Service
Information Integration					
Data Hub		●	●	●	●
Data Migration & Synchronization		●	●	●	●
Data Warehousing		●	●	●	●
Data Quality & Cleansing			○	○	○
Data Query & Reporting (BI)				●	●
Semantic Information Management			○	○	●
Business Process Integration					
Business Process Modelling	●	●	●	●	●
Business Process Management				●	●
Business Activity Monitoring				●	●
Business Process Analysis				○	○
Message Integration					
Message Queue		●	●	●	●
Publish/Subscribe Brokers		●	●	●	●
Application Adaptors		●	●	●	●
Element Management			●	●	●
Service Integration					
Web Services Development		●	●	●	●
Web Services Management		●	●	●	●
Software Frameworks & Libraries	●	●	●	●	●
Service Registry		●	●	●	●
Metadata and Repositories					
Application Portfolio			●	●	●
Enterprise Architecture	●	●	●	●	●
Configuration Management Database		○	○	●	●
Enterprise Data Model	●	●	●	●	●
Scanning Tools & Parsers				●	●

	Best Practices	Technology Services	Shared Services	Central Services	Self-Service
Other ICC Technologies					
Enterprise Information Portal (EIP)			●	●	●
XML Tools/Transformation		●	●	●	●
XML Vocabularies	○	○	○	○	●
B2B Integration Tools		●	●	●	●
e-Marketplace Private Exchanges		●	●	●	●

Figure 7-3. ICC Technology Catalog

The list is not exhaustive; there are hundreds of applications, integration standards, protocols, platforms, and suppliers in the market and thousands of specific products to satisfy various combinations and permutations of them. Furthermore, the ICC needs to manage and support legacy technologies, current offerings, and emerging capabilities.

Figure 7-3 identifies the core technology categories that are essential for each of the five ICC organizational models and those that are necessary for a progressive or advanced ICC. Core technologies are essential for any ICC. If you have not yet standardized on specific technologies in these areas across the enterprise, then you should do so before addressing any of the other categories.

Progressive technologies are recommended for ICCs operating at a maturity level of 2 or above (see Section 4.2 for details), but they may not be essential, depending on other factors such as the organization's size and the environment's complexity. The larger the organization and the more complex the environment, the more essential these technologies are.

The remainder of this chapter focuses on:

- Data integration technologies
- Application integration technologies
- The enterprise information portal
- The technology decision tree

7.1 Data Integration Technologies

Data integration technologies are primarily associated with integrating directly with application databases (DB2DB) rather than through application programming interfaces (APIs). Whenever possible, integrate applications through their supported APIs to provide a degree of decoupling between changes in the internal data models and to protect the integrity of the database when writing directly to it. The best data integration technologies today typically are able to integrate data at either the API or database layer. Sometimes performance or cost considerations make data integration at the database layer the most efficient option.

Some people might argue against using DB2DB technologies for integration because it conflicts with the loose-coupling principle. This is indeed the case in organizations that don't have standard data integration tools, haven't implemented a metadata repository, and don't have an enterprise data dictionary or data model. But more mature organizations—those that have implemented an ICC, leverage a data model, and use a metadata-driven integration platform—will be able to maintain the loose-coupling principle through the effective use of the technology and their processes to manage application changes.

Vendors who are basing integration at the data layer must support the concept of public interface tables. These tables serve as an established API and should be decoupled from the "black box" operational tables of the vendor's data architecture. Manage public interface tables the same as a component interface: clear documentation of versions, a slower life cycle (compared with the internal tables), use of principles of deprecation, and life-cycle communication for retirement of obsolete functionality.

Vendors providing data integration technologies at either the API or DB levels should also provide functionality for capturing only the data that has changed since the last load occurred. Often referred to as change data capture technology, this functionality furnishes a method for integrating data that is less resource intensive and more economical than other technology solutions that integrate an entire batch load of data during each execution.

7.1.1 Data Migration, Conversion, and Consolidation

Technologies that support data migration projects assist with large project efforts, such as system consolidation, legacy system conversion, and initial data loads for new application implementation.

These technologies generally use some form of ETL capabilities:

- **Extract:** Reads data from a source database and extracts a desired subset.

- **Transform:** Converts acquired data using rules, lookup tables, or creating combinations of data from multiple tables.

- **Load:** Writes the transformed data (either all of the subset or just the changes) to the target database.

7.1.2 Data Synchronization

Some projects require technologies that support a write-back capability to the source, thereby providing two-way synchronization. An appropriate technology provides write-back capability to the source through a set of virtual objects (sophisticated data models) that provide create-, read-, update-, and delete-style operations. Some of the systems also provide data access security enforced through an LDAP or registry-level tool. Data integration systems furnish persistence and transactional-level/OLTP-style updates by maintaining caches for the underlying batch systems.

7.1.3 Master Data Management

Master data management and reference data hubs employ ETL and Enterprise Information Integration (EII) technologies and provide a degree of persistence of the aggregated data in a central location. Loose coupling between applications is maintained through effective use of data models and a metadata-driven integration platform. Often these projects also utilize data cleansing technologies.

A master management system has many characteristics similar to data warehouses, but generally hubs are more focused—for example, providing a single view of customers, suppliers, products, or employees. They may also provide more online transactional processing (OLTP) for other applications that need to access common information in real time.

7.1.4 Data Warehousing

A data warehouse is a collection of data sourced from one or more application systems designed to support management decision making. Data warehouses contain a wide variety of data that presents a coherent picture of business conditions at a single point.

Development of a data warehouse includes developing systems to extract data from operating systems, plus installing a warehouse database system that gives managers flexible access to the data. Data in data warehouses needs to be integrated, subject oriented, stable, time variant, and enterprisewide.

In contrast to data warehouses, data marts are smaller subset repositories that serve the needs of particular user communities. Data warehouses and data marts are best represented using multidimensional models that can be sliced and diced, drilled down, and rolled up.

7.1.5 Data Quality and Cleansing

Data quality and cleaning tools help to remove errors, find inconsistencies, and identify missing information to improve the quality of data. Data cleaning is especially useful when integrating heterogeneous data sources, which may not uniformly have rigorous business rules or constraints around what kind of data may be entered into the system. Although some vendors refer to their products as data quality or information quality tools, they are more appropriately called data accuracy tools and may include such capabilities as checking names and addresses (including householding), duplicate records, and business rules.

7.1.6 Data Query and Reporting (BI)

Data query and reporting tools, also referred to as business intelligence (BI), take on many different forms from a wide variety of companies. The lines between the different types are increasingly blurred and may include production reports (invoicing), management reports (monthly sales), analytical reports (a comparison over time), and ad hoc reports. Some organizations will use one tool to do their ad hoc reporting, another tool (with a different interface) to call up their standard reports, and yet another tool if they want to write their own reports. The cost of incomplete or inefficiently generated intelligence can have a major impact on business operations, which means that effective technology in this arena can have a big payback.

The spectrum of data query and reporting technologies includes:

- Ad hoc queries
- Simple report formatting
- Sophisticated formatting
- Recurring production reports
- Slice-and-dice across hierarchical dimensions
- Charting and graphing
- Transforming data into images
- Visually exploring, digesting, and probing large quantities of data
- Uncovering predictive patterns
- Discovering hidden relationships locked inside data warehouses
- Forecasting future performance

Potential BI pitfalls that the ICC must pay attention to include no business intelligence standards, the "one vendor fits all" syndrome, failure to coordinate with the enterprise portal team, reporting from bad data, enterprise application analysis paralysis, lack of license management, no user auditing, and no retirement strategy.

7.1.7 Semantic Information Management

Semantic information management (SIM) includes tools for ontology modeling to support the creation of an information model, which should be compatible with entity-relationship and UML diagrams. It also handles mapping application data schemas to the central information model. SIM consists of a central integration repository and tools that significantly automate the collection, understanding, and use of metadata in data integration. It provides predefined interfaces for common systems and interchange standards, together with the ability to graphically map data from a wide range of file types, and automatically generates transformation code to run on different middleware platforms, as well as Java and XML-based environments.

The vision of SIM tools is to create an environment in which everyone speaks the same business language, data carries unambiguous business meaning, and the data environment is managed and integrated at will. Key elements of the architecture are metadata (knowing your data), an information model (knowing your business), and data semantics (understanding your data). Semantic information management creates value by delivering higher-quality business information, providing the flexibility to support business change, and making IT costs lower and more predictable. The technologies and standards in this arena are relatively new (for example, Semantic Web, OWL), so caution is recommended. SIM can be introduced gradually to specific projects and eventually extended to the entire enterprise.

7.2 Application Integration Technologies

We're often asked, "What integration technology should I use for my project?" It's no wonder this question comes up so often, given the vast array of tools (all able to solve any integration problem, according to vendors' claims), the competing industry standards, and the new buzzwords and alphabet soup of acronyms. It's very confusing.

In particular, beware of any "silver bullet" solutions. Practical experience has shown that while each tool may have a wide range of capabilities, each has its sweet spot. The challenge is to *consistently* select from the vast array of choices within the enterprise in the interests of simplifying a given IT infrastructure to drive down integration costs and risks. To begin, we need an integration architecture framework as outlined in Figure 7-4.

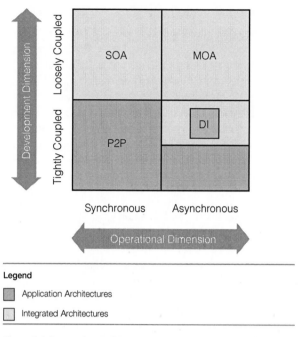

Figure 7-4. Integration Architectures

In our framework, SOA stands for service oriented architecture and includes Web services and enterprise service bus (ESB) technologies. MOA, or message oriented architecture, includes message queuing, integration brokers and publish/subscribe capabilities. FTP, or other file-based protocols, are also included in this category—a file is simply a form of a message—albeit without as much functionality as most messaging protocols. DI stands for data integration, which includes data warehouse, ETL, and federated repository technologies. P2P stands for point-to-point solutions and encompasses a vast range of development tools and system protocols.

The vertical dimension distinguishes between tightly coupled and loosely coupled development architectures. Loosely coupled means that one component can change without impacting another component. For example, if a source system were to add several new data elements to a message and the target systems were not required to change as a result (unless they wanted to use the new elements), they would be loosely coupled. By definition, a loosely coupled approach is an *integration architecture,* while a tightly coupled approach is an *application architecture*.

You will notice that the DI approach in Figure 7-4 is both an integration architecture and an application architecture. The maturity of DI platforms and their ability to share metadata across different applications has enabled databases from different applications to be tightly coupled yet evolve independently. However, there are two key constraints for this to hold true: (1) the systems being integrated must both be within the same trusted domain (typically within the same enterprise group and with no firewall issues), and (2) the architects of the systems involved must collaborate very closely. If these two conditions do not exist in a given situation, the DI approaches should be classified as application architectures.

On the horizontal dimension, "synchronous" refers to a request/reply pattern where the source system is blocked from making the next execution step until it receives a response from the target system. Asynchronous patterns, on the other hand, are either batch driven or event driven, but the events are handled as another processing thread in parallel with whatever other processing the system is performing. (A "batch" job is simply a special case of an event—one that is driven by the clock in a particular repeating, time-driven pattern.)

As is often the case in integration, there are no absolutes. At the lowest level, packet-based network architectures, such as TCP/IP, are essentially asynchronous, compared with circuit-switched architectures. Asynchronous approaches, if designed appropriately, can be used to implement certain request/reply patterns. Two one-way, back-to-back queued message flows between systems can look very similar to a single SOAP Web service call. For example, a credit authorization at a point-of-sale (POS) terminal may send a message to an input queue of an integration broker. The broker distributes it on a first-in/first-out basis to one of several credit bureaus, which then sends a message back through the broker to the POS system. Nevertheless, the distinction between synchronous and asynchronous is useful and widely accepted in software engineering discussions.

In summary, these two dimensions that consider both the development phase and the operational phase of systems divide the landscape into four broad architecture categories. When coupled with the legacy of a given enterprise and a conscious decision concerning how to best limit choices to simplify an integration environment, they can form the basis of a technology decision tree (see Section 7.4).

7.2.1 Message Oriented Integration

The primary purpose of integration brokers and other message oriented middleware is to enable systems that were independently developed, with different technologies, and that remain independently managed, to inter-operate. Message oriented architecture (MOA) allows individual systems to change independently of each other, yet still function in an end-to-end business process. For the overall enterprise infrastructure to be truly adaptive requires a robust MOA infrastructure that allows each component to adapt as quickly as it can with minimal coordination and dependence on other components.

MOA systems also support flexibility by "homogenizing" interface standards and event information. This capability is an important enabler for enterprise BAM and BPM because while these solutions can be done in the absence of a message oriented architecture, they may require many custom point adapters or translators, which can drive up costs and the fragility of the solution.

MOA systems generally have three key elements: adapters, message queues, and brokers. Adapters are software elements that transform data from one form to another and translate one protocol into another. For example, an adapter may read data in XML format from an interface using a JMS protocol and write it as a comma-delimited ASCII format to a file that is then transmitted using an FTP. In addition, adapters may be used to encrypt data, compress or group messages, or perform other complex transformations. Message queues are software elements that provide a first-in/first-out queuing mechanism with message persistence until it is delivered, or read. Brokers may supply a wide variety of functionality depending on the product, but essentially they are intended to support publish/subscribe or multicast capabilities.

In addition, integration brokers may provide transformation capabilities and system-to-human and human-to-human process management to their suite of offerings. This additional capability for handling business processes involving people has generally been available only in workflow and pure-play BPM offerings. Organizations with a mature integration framework should consider their vendor's BPM offerings to leverage the integration potential within a single vendor stack.

Many excellent products are on the market that support one or all of the MOA components. Alternatively, open source options are also available, including openadapter (www.openadapter.org) and Open-JMS.

7.2.2 Service Oriented Integration

A service oriented architecture (SOA) is an architectural strategy that seeks to segment and isolate critical application and data functionality and access into small, operationally independent pieces that can be executed remotely and in a highly distributed manner. The end goal of service oriented architecture is to provide easy and secure access to enterprise technology and process resources, maximizing reuse and minimizing cost while improving the performance and reliability of these systems. An SOA encapsulates business logic for consistent results across applications, accommodates ease of change, provides better control over data sources through an abstraction layer, and makes integration in a heterogeneous environment easier.

An SOA is an important consideration because, unlike traditional systems architecture, it starts with the assumption that functional components are stateless objects that a separate and independent process management layer will control. Traditional systems that were designed as holistic stand-alone systems in their own right require special treatment when used within a larger enterprise end-to-end solution.

Interestingly, precursors to SOA occur in well-managed mainframe environments' use of CICS to decouple key transactions from their encapsulating application logic, promoting reuse and transactional integrity.

7.2.3 Business Process Integration

The current state of the business-process landscape is confusing. Acronyms abound with conflicting definitions, and industry analysts and technology companies continue to compound the problem. BPM is used to describe business-process modeling, business-process monitoring, and business-performance management. BAM is used to describe both business activity modeling and business activity monitoring, and BPA can describe business process architecture or business-process analysis.

BAM, BPM, and Workflow are tricky terms because they are overused "buzz words," and various interest groups tend to put their own spin on them. Workflow, business-process management, and business rules engines seem to be used interchangeably. Although Workflow has been around for several years, the differentiators between Workflow and business-process management are unclear.

A useful breakdown of the primary process analysis and modeling, development, execution, and monitoring domains is as follows:

- **Business process analysis (BPA)** includes analysis, modeling, and simulation of business processes.

- **Business process management (BPM)** includes development, run-time execution, and monitoring of business process within its span of control. BPM also includes IS-assisted human-to-human Workflow.

- **Business activity monitoring (BAM)** includes monitoring of business events within and across processes regardless of their execution environment.

Although BPM tools provide some BAM capabilities, they are generally limited to the process context managed by the BPM engine because they may not have visibility outside the context that they control. Another way to think of BAM and BPM is on a spectrum, with the two ends having the following characteristics:

BAM	BPM
Passive process control	Active process control
Nonlinear event recognition	Linear defined sequences
Reacting to out-of-bound events	Controlling and directing events
Leverages event architecture	Leverages service oriented architecture

Figure 7-5. BAM and BPM Comparison

The critical aspect of business process integration to highlight here is that it is not a replacement for SOA or MOA; rather, it acts as an additional integration "layer" that can leverage messaging architectures or service architects to orchestrate long-running business processes or to group multiple individual transactions into a logical unit of work. If you approach BPM from this perspective, it will help to eliminate the confusion with MOA and SOA.

References: Adaptive Business Process Management

7.3 Enterprise Information Portal (EIP)

There is a dizzying array of companies in the enterprise portal space, ranging from enterprise software stalwarts, such as SAP and Siebel, through infrastructure giants, such as IBM and Sun, to pure-plays such as BroadVision and Plumtree. However, the core functionality remains largely the same across vendors: It is a platform that aggregates information, applications, and processes and delivers them to internal and external users.

Typically a vendor's offering will include a core portal engine along with features such as application integration, collaboration, search, business intelligence, and content management. Personalization is the enterprise portal's key functionality, which involves adapting the display of information and processes to a user's preference, behavior, location, role, language, device, and channel.

Our intention in this book is not to try to make sense of the vast array of rapidly changing portal technologies, but rather to recognize their importance and role in the ICC as a key technology to enable "integration at the glass." At a minimum, every ICC, from the best-practices model through the self-service model, should plan to implement an integration portal. It's basically the central authority within the enterprise for information concerning integration. Figure 7-6 shows a real-life example of such a portal.

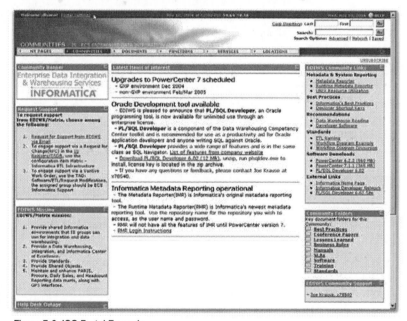

Figure 7-6. ICC Portal Example

7.4 Technology Decision Tree

To help cut through the rhetoric and to provide consistency for how technologies are used, we recommend that each ICC develop for itself an integration technology decision tree. There is no off-the-shelf formula for this because every organization has a legacy of tools, technology, and staff experience that must be factored into the decision tree. For a decision tree to be useful it must discriminate between competing choices and it must result in specific tool selections.

The biggest value is having a decision tree that is applied consistently across the enterprise. It is less important what the actual technologies are, because integration is more about gaining agreement among disparate teams than about building a theoretically ideal architecture. A decision tree that deals only with conceptual integration architectures without specifying products (or internally developed tools) by name is of limited value. There are so many ways to interpret abstract architectures that everyone could comply with them, but you could still end up with a hairball in production.

Figure 7-7 is an example of what a decision tree for a specific enterprise might look like. In real life, making decisions can be more complex because there are often technical or political mitigating circumstances. The intent is that the decision tree can help project teams decide on the appropriate technology in 80 percent of the situations. The ICC architects or an architecture review board can handle the remaining 20 percent of special cases.

In this example, the ICC has standardized on open adapter (an open source software framework) for all its message-based integrations. Note that there are various ways to configure the framework to include multiple subscribers to common message topics, remove the XML transformations to optimize performance, and configure it as a point-to-point interface when appropriate.

In addition, this ICC has standardized on Informatica for Web services (SOA) and Informatica® PowerCenter™ for ETL. Furthermore, the Informatica PowerChannel™ tools are the standard of choice for any file-based movement of information, whether inside the enterprise or externally with customers and suppliers.

There is one final consideration for the decision tree: To be complete, it must also have a defined exception process. People will accept a set of standards (rules) much more readily if there is a way to bypass them. This idea may seem counterintuitive, but to gain acceptance of a set of standards, provide an easy exit path and you'll find that people will be much more willing to try it. Once everyone understands and trusts the standards, then the exception process becomes increasingly unnecessary.

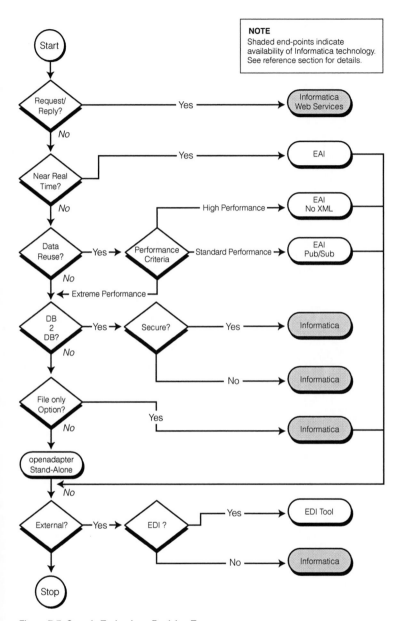

Figure 7-7. Sample Technology Decision Tree

ICC Technology

Chapter 8

Advanced Concepts in Integration

Remember that just because something is a "best practice" doesn't mean that it's any good. Bloodletting was considered a best practice in the medical field for hundreds of years until the body's circulatory system was fully understood. We must keep in mind that computer science as a discipline and information management as a profession are quite immature in comparison to other professions such as accounting, law, engineering, and medicine. And integration, as a subspecialty within information management, is even more immature, with only about 20 years under its belt.

It is clear, however, that computer technology advances are not going to stop and that the free market economy will continue to drive new innovations. The net result is that information complexity will continue to increase and so the hierarchy of systems will continue to grow.

We have much "growing up" to do and it will be many years before the disciplines of integration can approach the level of maturity we expect from other professions. The research and academic communities, however, are paying more and more attention to the issues of integration. It is only a matter of time before fundamental theories are developed, and are experimentally validated, so we can build practices using truly proven theories. For example, very few universities offer graduate degrees in integration (it may be possible to count them on one hand), but the fact that there any at all is significant.

The sections in this chapter delve into several areas of scientific research and philosophical inquiry that provide some useful perspectives on where the future of integration may land. Most of this chapter is based on articles published between 2001 and 2004 in the "Software Ecologist" column of the *Business Integration Journal*. We have selected and edited them for this book because of their forward-looking perspective and thought-provoking orientation.

8.1 Complex Adaptive Systems

Between the sixteenth and eighteenth centuries, there was a dramatic shift in the way Western people observed and thought about the universe. This new system of thought was based on the philosophy of Rene Descartes, who promoted a mathematical description of nature and the use of analytic thought, known as the Cartesian system. Descartes's vision was to give a precise and complete account of all natural phenomena with absolute mathematical certainty. To accomplish this, he compared natural phenomena with machines. Descartes even drew parallels between a sick man and an ill-made clock. Isaac Newton later synthesized the works of Copernicus, Kepler, Galileo, and Descartes into a complete mathematical formulation of nature: Newtonian mechanics. Toward the end of the nineteenth century, scientists believed that eventually all natural phenomena would be explained by reducing them to the motion and interaction of particles. Reductionism led to the expectation that:

- Physics would eventually explain chemistry,
- Chemistry would explain biology, and
- Biology would explain psychology.

Thus love, joy, and inspiration were reduced to the interaction between atoms in the brain.

These schools of thought help us understand the tension between rationalism—knowledge deduced mathematically from first principles—and empiricism—knowledge that has been cross-checked in the external world. The idea of "checking your work" is significant in both Cartesian and Newtonian thought, but the mechanics of validation are quite different. In the Cartesian approach, truth is guaranteed by the logical correctness of deductive thought; in the Newtonian approach, experiment decides truth. This distinction is extremely relevant today in software engineering, which is rooted in the deductive approach of Descartes. Our position is that we need a lot more Newton in our thinking.

At the dawn of the twentieth century, the universe was no longer seen as a machine, made up of a multitude of separate parts, but as a harmonious indivisible whole. Organismic biology, for example, emphasized the view of living organisms as integrated wholes whose properties cannot be reduced to those of the smaller parts. The famous saying, "The whole is more than the sum of its parts," was coined by gestalt psychologists who discovered that living organisms do not perceive things in terms of isolated elements but as integrated perceptual patterns.

Ecologists who focused on the study of animal and plant communities observed networks of relationships—the web of life. They found a new way of thinking in terms of relationships, connectedness, and context. According to Fritjof Capra:

> "We may call this ecological thinking, or systems thinking. It is based on the fundamental shift of perception from the world as a machine to the world as a living system. This shift concerns our perception of nature, of the human organism, and of society."

> "Systems thinking involves shifting our attention from the parts to the whole, from objects to relationships, from structures to processes, from hierarchies to networks. It also includes shifts of emphasis from the rational to the intuitive, from analysis to synthesis, from linear to nonlinear thinking."

We wholeheartedly agree with Capra, especially about shifting our thought centers from objects and structures to relationships and processes. The consequences of this transition in IT, if it ever happens, will be enormous because most of the practical doctrine that we have built up over the past 15 to 20 years will have to be scrapped. From information engineering on, the emphasis has been on locating the essence of the enterprise system portfolio in the data model—a structural view of essence. This view is seductive because enterprise data models are durable and stable, but mistaking this durability for essence is equivalent to considering the fossilized bones of dinosaurs their essence. In fact, we know that the bones of an organism, far from being the essence of the living thing, are instead the durable—but largely incidental—part that endures through the ages.

The enterprise application portfolio is the organizational memory, the fossil, of the decisions and actions that business and IT have acquired over time. To pass on more than fossils to the next generation of IS professionals, we should take a few lessons from history. Specifically, we urge: Focus on process (the essence of complex adaptive systems) first and data second, attack problems holistically and avoid fragmented point solutions, and test proposed solutions—not just analytical models—in the real world.

8.2 The Philosophy of Integration

According to Buddhist philosophy, all phenomena depend on other phenomena, which are themselves dependent on other phenomena, and so on. No matter how deep or far back we search, no phenomenon is fundamental or a "thing—in itself." In addition, neither the observer nor the observed phenomenon exists independently—each is inextricably intertwined. Buddhists believe that all phenomena depend on three things:

1. Their causes (gross dependent relationship)

2. Their parts (subtle dependent relationship)

3. Their imputation by the mind of a sentient being (very subtle dependent relationship)

To Buddhists, all things lack a defining essence—they are in a constant state of impermanence, becoming and decaying. Phenomena are never found; rather, they exist only in terms of other things, such as the mind that generates those definitions.

For example, everyone knows what a car is, but what makes it a car is surprisingly difficult to pin down. At what stage on the production line do the various parts become a car? Does my car temporarily cease to be a car when it's in the shop and the transmission is physically removed? Is it still a car when I wake up to find it supported on bricks and the wheels stolen? Is the essential feature of a car the fact that it performs the functions of a car?

The *causes* of a car are the geological processes that produced coal and iron and copper ores, followed by the miners, metalworkers, designers, component manufacturers, and assembly line workers who transformed the raw material into the finished product. These causes are objective, existing independently from our participation.

The *parts* of a car are more nebulous. We can view a car as being composed of a chassis, an engine, and four wheels. Or we can take a more detailed view, seeing the engine as pistons, a cylinder head, a carburetor, and so on. Each of these parts can be analyzed into subcomponents, from atoms of iron and carbon to fundamental particles such as protons, electrons, and the photons that shine from the headlamps. How we choose to subdivide the whole determines our perception of parts.

By now you're probably wondering what this discussion has to do with systems integration. Following are three examples aligned with the three levels of dependent relationships.

We know that enterprise frameworks and reference models are essential elements of an integration architecture. But many frameworks offer a dizzying array of models in a complex matrix of views and domains. Which models are the most important? Where do we start? Buddhist philosophy would suggest starting with the process dimension rather than the traditional systems or data-driven dimension. Of the three levels of dependent relationships in the complex world of modern systems integration, processes (causal relationships) are the most objective and least subject to debate. So the cornerstone for your integration solution should be an end-to-end process model.

A second example deals with structural issues such as system hierarchies or data models. Our training and education steer us down a path of analytical decomposition to find the one "right" solution in this context. These teachings are based on the Western philosophies of Plato and the science of Descartes, Newton, and others. Yet, as in the car example, how exactly do we define an application or system, and when do we know we have the "right" data model? The definition of these structural views depends on many subtle relationships. Although the common Western view is that structure in software systems is solid and should be "engineered," Buddhism suggests that *everything* is based on outside factors and is constantly morphing. Maybe we should engineer our processes and let the systems and data evolve from them?

The final example deals with the slippery issue of semantics. Anyone who has tried to create a canonical data model knows how difficult it is to gain a common understanding of even such simple attributes as customer, account, or address. Syntax issues are structural (customer_abc versus customer_123), and somewhat easier, but semantics issues deal with data's "meaning." Each of us has a unique perspective based on our experience, which has a *direct* impact on the meaning of data. Once again, a Buddhist perspective can help us recognize that there is no "perfect" data model. Because events are tied to processes (the most objective of all dependent relationships), we have a much better chance of developing a practical solution if we focus on developing a canonical *event* model instead.

Portions of this section are extracted from a collection of essays on modern Buddhism, philosophy, and science. We encourage you to explore these essays further at http://home.btclick.com/scimah/. Although a dose of Zen may not solve all your integration challenges, you might find yourself transcending to a higher state of understanding and peaceful well-being in a world of subtle and often incomprehensible dependencies.

8.3 Chaos Theory in Integration

At the December 1972 meeting of the American Association for the Advancement of Science in Washington, DC, Edward Lorenz gave a talk entitled, "Predictability: Does the Flap of a Butterfly's Wings in Brazil Set Off a Tornado in Texas?" Lorenz was speaking about work he started many years earlier concerning chaotic systems in which a small change in initial conditions produces wildly different results. In chaotic systems, the simple, deterministic dynamics of components combine to create irregular, random-looking behavior.

Examples of chaotic behavior are everywhere in large-scale integrated IT environments. The following are just a few of the possibilities:

- A security group tightens up controls by changing database access passwords, and a call center application with a previously unknown dependency on the database suddenly fails.

- An entire supply chain process collapses when a server under an analyst's desk is shut down.

- A minor security patch is applied to the operating system of an application server, resulting in incorrect inventory replenishment orders two weeks later.

- A customer data item that is left blank is handled properly by the ordering, fulfillment, and billing applications and then fails when the collections application processes it one month later.

These examples surely exhibit chaotic behavior, but are the systems really chaotic? Is the behavior simply the result of insufficient and inadequate knowledge of the relationships between dependent components in a complex environment? If only our software vendors could articulate the impact of their new release changes more completely. If only we had a more complete and up-to-date configuration management database (CMDB). If only the test environment was identical to the production environment so that we could conduct a more comprehensive integration test before making production changes.

Unfortunately, a certain amount of unpredictability and chaos is inevitable in the integration discipline. Integration, by definition, is the process of taking applications that were independently developed, may use incompatible technology, and remain independently managed, and then making them work together. When it comes to vendors, there should be a sixth integration law: *Vendors will do what they damn well please.*

Furthermore, to maintain a complete and accurate CMDB, we should remember the theoretical work of W. Ross Ashby on effective regulation. He showed that an *effective, independent controlling system must include (or "be") a full working model of any system it controls.*

We could concede the futility of ultimate control—the reality of chaos—and simply live with a certain amount of unpredictability. If we choose this path, then we are choosing to operate our integration infrastructure in the same manner as the macroeconomics and weather forecasting disciplines operate. However, the idea of running a large, fiscally responsible, accountable corporation based on "probabilities" is nerve-racking. Although Ashby's insight suggests that a certain amount of chaos will always be present, there is much we can do to gain control over independently developed and maintained applications.

In fact, we can use the chaos theory to our advantage. In the book *Seven Life Lessons of Chaos,* John Briggs and F. David Peat call this "Butterfly Power: How to Let Chaos Grow Local Efforts into Global Results." The idea is to make small, calculated actions that will—over time—have a large impact. There are plenty of opportunities to apply this principle in any large IS organization, but the biggest one may be in the ICC. For example, establishing interface standards and a governance process to ensure that they are followed for newly deployed applications can have a huge impact on driving down integration costs, improving quality, and reducing production "surprises" over time. This leverage is substantially increased with an ICC because it is the "glue" connecting all the other applications in the enterprise.

Hence the butterfly is a powerful inspiration. A beautiful, innocuous-looking insect, the butterfly makes small movements: well calculated, supremely strategic, and tremendously influential over time. Unlike elephant-size applications or 500-pound-gorilla ERP systems, the power of the ICC is in small, strategic changes whose importance unfolds gradually. And while you might need a little patience to wait for the results, they are likely to be as rewarding—even beautiful—as watching that caterpillar turn into a butterfly.

8.4 The Rule of Eminent Domain

The challenges of integration have often been compared to city planning. The rule of eminent domain may be a good case study. The power that governments can wield to seize and redevelop property for the common good offers some suggestions for practices that may well be applicable in optimizing enterprise IT infrastructures. Here is one example.

Located 30 miles northwest of Boston, Lowell, Massachusetts, was the United States' first planned industrial city, which grew in significance during America's Industrial Revolution. After World War I, Lowell, along with most northern industrial cities, slid into decline as manufacturing companies migrated to the south. Decades of disinvestment and decay followed and the term "brownfields" emerged to describe the acres of brown-brick industrial buildings. With the land almost completely developed and with historic industrial buildings standing adjacent to high-density residential neighborhoods, Lowell was faced with a critical shortage of land and the modern industrial space needed to attract job-producing businesses.

More than 40 percent of the buildings within a 113-acre planning area were deteriorated, in need of major repair, or unfit for human habitation. The diversity of individual site ownership, irregular lot sizes, and obsolete street patterns made it highly unlikely that this area would ever be redeveloped through the unaided efforts of private enterprise. Brownfields require not only assembling land from fragmented, underutilized parcels, but also cleaning up toxic contamination, an issue that can be a black hole both financially and in terms of regulation.

Lowell's downward trend has since been reversed, thanks to major restoration projects undertaken by the city, assistance from the Environmental Protection Agency, and the rule of eminent domain. Eminent domain is the power of government agencies to acquire property for public use. Recognized public uses include, among other things, schools, parks, roads, highways, subways, fire and police stations, public buildings such as libraries, and the elimination of blight through redevelopment. A key attribute of eminent domain is that the government can exercise this power even if the owner does not wish to sell his or her property.

The Fifth Amendment of the U.S. Constitution and Article I, Section 19, of the California Constitution allow private property to be taken by eminent domain for a "public use." The courts have interpreted this term very broadly and the project need not be actually open to the public to constitute a public use. Instead, only a public benefit is generally required. Elimination of blight through redevelopment projects, for example, is a public benefit that courts have held satisfies the "public use" requirement of the federal and state constitutions.

The challenges of redeveloping legacy integration infrastructures have parallels with redevelopment of legacy industrial brownfields. Fragmented interfaces, irregular data definitions, and inconsistent operational standards that grew rapidly in the 1980s and 1990s as the result of project silos working with constantly changing technology have left behind an integration landscape that is, quite simply, a mess. The equivalent IT term for industrial brownfields is integration hairballs. And while the integration infrastructure may not exactly be "toxic," it presents similar challenges in terms of cleanup and has the potential of becoming a budgetary black hole.

For IS departments to tackle these challenges and have some hope of resolving them, CIOs need to empower enterprise architecture groups and integration competency centers (ICCs) with the equivalent powers of eminent domain. Architects need support from the top of the organization to be able to define and enforce enterprise standards. And ICCs need to be able to approach application teams and say, "These application interfaces are no longer 'yours.' They are now the responsibility of the ICC and will be redeveloped according to enterprise standards to maximize reuse and to reduce operating costs."

Countries might not function well without the power of eminent domain. Yet the idea that the government can have such power over private property is often frightening and frustrating to landowners. A landowner whose farm may be lost or torn apart by a highway project will likely be overwhelmed by the power of eminent domain. There's no guarantee that all the brownfields in America will ever be cleaned up and reused productively. But the emerging trend suggests a new generation of urban redevelopment that's likely to have a big impact.

Companies also would not function well without the equivalent power of eminent domain. In fact, this power exists in the hands of senior executives and is often applied to many aspects of the operation. It's time we recognized that interfaces between applications are not the domain of the applications, but rather the domain of the whole. We need to treat integration elements as shared enterprise systems that have their own life cycle independent of the application systems they serve. Making this shift will require some gut-wrenching changes for organizations as some power shifts from application teams to architecture and ICC teams, but if we ever want to untangle the integration hairball, these changes are necessary.

8.5 Valuing Enterprise Architecture

A common debate in many IT projects is whether to spend extra time and money to build a flexible solution or to implement a point solution that meets the immediate needs. This debate can be a big source of tension between IT and business. Business leaders see a market opportunity and are motivated to implement a solution quickly that meets immediate needs. IT staff have been "burned" in the past by implementing point solutions and then later getting blamed when the solution turns out be expensive to maintain and hard to change.

Enterprise architecture (EA) as an approach is a way to address this issue and close the gap between business and IT. However, the current heuristic-based approach to EA, though useful, has drawbacks. Links between architectural concepts and business decisions are often qualitative, weak, and subjective. The architectural concepts focus more on "how to structure the enterprise components" rather than "how to increase organizational value."

Many organizations view EA as an activity to lower total cost of ownership (TCO) rather than as a way to maximize value added to the enterprise. This misconception is clear from the predominance of investment decision methods focused on short-term payback and cost elimination and technically oriented architectures rather than business-oriented architectures. EA initiatives should make value enhancement their primary objective rather than technical perfection.

Virtually all large organizations use formal processes for creating business cases for IT investments that, theoretically, provide the mechanism for making good enterprise decisions. The problem with most business case methods is that they are biased toward tactical decisions. In short, there is no way to express architectural flexibility as numerical values that can be plugged into a spreadsheet.

Traditional ROI methods such as net present value (NPV), internal rate of return, payback period, or economic value added are not ideal for EA initiatives. These methods are sound, proven techniques that succeed with well-defined problems where the risks and options are clearly understood and stable. But they do not consider the greatest value that an enterprise architecture investment provides—namely, creating an adaptive infrastructure that can change rapidly in the future in response to new business needs or new technology developments.

All of the standard ROI techniques stress measuring the cost and revenue impact of a given investment, but none of them includes a factor for flexibility, perhaps the most important factor in a modern, fast-paced competitive environment. The net result is that short-term, rapid payback IT investments take priority over long-term strategic enabling infrastructures.

Granted, some ROI techniques consider risk management and flexibility, albeit as soft (subjective) factors. The balanced scorecard methodology is one of the best known of such techniques and is summarized here:

> "Balanced scorecard provides a set of principles and analytic techniques for improving an organization's performance in four general areas: financials, customers, learning, and internal processes. This approach is potentially all-encompassing, combining financial and nonfinancial goals and measures. Balanced scorecard is future-oriented, not a rearview mirror on performance."

Gary Anthes, *ComputerWorld, ROI Guide,* 2003

On the downside, the balanced scorecard approach is potentially so broad that it may divert attention from the key factors that are vital to shareholder return. It doesn't readily weigh the relative importance of the different metrics, and many of the nonfinancial components may be subjective.

An alternative method exists, however, that factors in the adaptability of an enterprise architecture from a quantitative perspective. The real-options approach applies sophisticated mathematical models to measure the business value of enterprise architectures. It applies concepts from financial options theory to investments such as manufacturing plants or IT infrastructure. Similar to financial stock options, companies that make strategic investments have the right, but not the obligation, to exploit future investments.

Real options can take a number of forms, such as these examples:

- The company can exercise the option to expand its commitment to a strategy. For example, the company may build an infrastructure to support offshore call centers that could be easily expanded to other business areas if the strategy works out well.

- An initial investment may serve as a platform to grow the company into new business areas. For example, exposing the functionality of internal ordering systems to the Internet through Web services could create a portfolio of real options to extend business operations into a variety of new markets.

- Management may begin with a relatively small trial investment and create an option to abandon the project if results are unsatisfactory. Pilot projects isolated in one geography or one product line are good examples of this trial method.

Conceptually, the real-options approach makes a lot of sense. To take a simple example, let's say you have two options:

- Buy a two-server system for $50,000 to meet your immediate needs, with each subsequent two-server expansion costing $50,000 and requiring one month lead time to install.

- Buy a larger frame with two server blades at $70,000 that can easily be expanded to up to 16 servers by simply plugging in new blades one at a time for $20,000 each and requiring only one week of lead time.

The better decision is not obvious because there are risks related to the efficiency of the application and how rapidly the application workload will increase. Both of these factors are unknowns and can impact how many servers need to be added and when. In the first scenario, you may end up paying more in the long run, but you won't tie up as much capital up front.

In the second scenario, the initial investment creates value by allowing smaller incremental future investments and by letting those decisions be made later, presumably therefore with better information and lower risks.

Real options is a promising approach for quantifying the risks, uncertainty, and alternatives inherent in IT architectural trade-offs, but it is still a new method with few case studies available. But for organizations that are willing to experiment with new techniques, real options can help articulate the value of enterprise architecture in a way that allows business, finance, and IT to speak a common language. The net result should be better decisions, more realistic expectations, and ultimately greater value to the enterprise.

8.5.1 How EA Is Often Undervalued

Imagine this scenario: The VP of marketing plays a round of golf with the CEO of a software company that has an innovative cross-sell tool and gets excited about the tool's impact on market share at other companies. Back at the office, the VP has the marketing staff perform an analytical study and quickly concludes that the solution will drive $20 million in incremental sales in the current fiscal year—and it needs to be implemented only in one channel and one product line within three months before the annual peak in the customer buying cycle. The cross-sell CEO says his company can implement the entire solution for $2 million. Sounds like a "no brainer," right?

However, when the enterprise architect looks at the solution, it becomes apparent that (1) the cross-sell tool runs on an operating system platform that is new to the company, (2) the internal database is a proprietary data model that is difficult to map to other customer systems, and (3) if the solution were to be extended later to all channels and all products, it would be 10 times bigger than the largest current installation anywhere (read "high risk") and would cost many millions to fully integrate into the company's operational systems. Furthermore, the architect says that IT has been anticipating this need for the past year and has already surveyed the market for off-the-shelf solutions and concluded that none of them fit well into the current infrastructure. He then pulls out a thick slide deck to show marketing the robust architecture model for the development of an in-house solution that would be efficient, leverage all the company's current systems, and be scalable to support all products, channels, and geographies—but it will take 12 months to implement.

We know how this plays out because it's such a common pattern. The VP of marketing controls the purse strings and his bonus is tied to achieving the sales targets. When the finance people get involved and prepare the business case, the ROI shows a clear six-month payback. The project goes ahead and is a terrific success, so the following year the business wants to roll the solution out across the entire company. The IT staff puts in a valiant effort to scale the solution, but because of integration issues and performance problems, the project grows into a two-year nightmare of escalating costs, missed expectations, tired and frustrated IT staff, and unhappy business executives. In the end, the solution works, but it's a fragile operation that chews up more than its share of the maintenance budget and is hard to change for the next marketing initiative.

8.5.2 Increase Uncertainty to Lower Risks

We have adapted the following text, with permission, from *Real Options Perspective to Enterprise Architecture as an Investment Activity,* by Dr. Pallab Saha, Institute of Systems Science, National University of Singapore.

The flexibility an enterprise has to incorporate changes depends on its structure. Changing and uncertain future business conditions make the capability to incorporate changes necessary. Thus flexibility offers great value and is a desirable characteristic that can buffer against downside risks as well as exposure to upside opportunity. The ability to call off an initiative early in the life cycle in light of unfavorable new information minimizes the risk, while the flexibility to adapt the enterprise to take advantage of new business opportunities provides upside potential. Flexibility as an organizational capability is gaining increasing importance in areas of architectural thinking.

The dilemma most organizations face is that while the costs involved in building for flexibility are largely tangible, the value is hard to quantify, elusive, and largely intangible. This intangibility results because potential payoffs from flexibility occur in the future, contingent on uncertain future conditions. This uncertainty fuels the need for organizations to have an approach that allows comparison of real (tangible) costs to real (tangible) value by making the present value of flexibility tangible.

Traditional approaches in investment analysis fail to capture flexibility, risks, and contingencies that have the potential to impact business decisions. Static NPV, for example, is generally not a good measure for valuing an enterprise because it tends to overlook one of the key sources of value: the flexibility of the enterprise to adapt to newly discovered and dynamic information, markets, and environments.

The three main approaches to help make the value of flexibility tangible include: (1) dynamic discounted cash flow analysis, (2) decision analysis (using utility theory), and (3) real options. Each approach is appropriate under certain conditions and has its strengths and weaknesses. The real-options approach is more suitable and has wider applicability than the others within the context of EA investments.

In statistical decision theory, risk is defined as "the expected value of a loss function." It is critical to note that (1) risk arises from choice, (2) risk is a probabilistic phenomenon, and (3) uncertainty is the source of risk.

Increasing uncertainty can actually reduce risks and vice versa. This phenomenon can be explained by the fact that uncertainty and complexity are closely linked and produce an undesirable side effect for decision makers, which is lack of precision. This link has been formalized as the law of incompatibility, which states that "as complexity increases, precise statements lose meaning and meaningful statements lose precision." This statement means that increasing uncertainty in the decision-making process and associated analyses to better reflect true uncertainty actually lowers risk. In other words, ignoring complexity or uncertainty is risky.

Uncertainty and the value of flexibility in the face of uncertainty are at the core of both enterprise architecture development and finance. Reducing risk by introducing uncertainty is what real options are about, and it uses Monte Carlo methods that perform computerized statistical sampling experiments to achieve this goal. In contrast to traditional methods based on discounted cash flow, where uncertainty about possible future implementation opportunities is penalized, the real-options approach acknowledges the existence of risks and uncertainties and allows investments to be configured accordingly.

8.6 Advanced Concepts in Metadata

A full-service integration competency center has certain infrastructure requirements to provide a scalable and predictable level of service across the architect/design/build/deploy/operate/manage life cycle. These requirements include:

- System-to-system data flow maps

- Detailed and searchable schemas for all data flows

- Middleware configuration management: how components interact with the messaging infrastructure

A "metadata" system is necessary to meet these requirements. Use of metadata is an established industry practice in larger IT organizations. It started off with basic "data dictionaries," which documented the business meaning of data elements, and evolved into a general inventory of data, programs, and other IT assets. It has significant overlaps with IT asset management and configuration management, and there is a general lack of consensus in the IT industry about the relative scope of these disciplines.

In the context of a full-service ICC, metadata faces challenges because fully and accurately documenting the integrations between an enterprise's systems is difficult. Robust processes and information models are required, and there are few, if any, generally accepted best practices.

The general issues of metadata are:

- The need for a service-centric foundation
- Logical to physical traceability
- Dependency management

The remainder of this chapter will drill into some of the hands-on challenges.

8.6.1 The Need for a Service-Centric Foundation

Managing the detailed metadata for an integration competency center requires a conceptual framework. Enterprise application integration implies that one is managing the problem from a perspective of application to application, not database to database. What is the significance of this perspective? It's a conceptual evolution, calling for a focus on applications as unitary, encapsulated services, rather than the glass-box nature of shared databases. This focus is consistent with important trends in current IT:

- Increasing deployments of packages of services replacing home-built software. Database schemas (as the package vendor's proprietary concern) often become opaque and irrelevant in a packaged software world.

- The emergence of IT service management as a foundational IT process concept: What does the application (as IT service) do for the business?

- The increasing momentum behind service oriented architecture. This again calls for encapsulation of system internals behind well-defined interfaces.

8.6.2 Basics of System

What do we mean by a "system"? You might overhear the following in the halls of Fortune 500 IT shops every day:

"PLV is down!"

"Quadrex isn't talking to the IC hub!"

"We're doing a capacity upgrade on the NST databases."

"The X-time batch was two hours late today."

What does such gibberish mean?

Such conversations are the hallmark of the modern enterprise IT shop. The acronyms and abbreviations are managerial shorthand for large collections of IT components, usually grouped together in service of particular business purposes. These abstractions are essential to managing the complexity of a large IT environment, simplifying otherwise impossibly verbose conversations into pithy exchanges hooking together the technical and business worlds.

What are these things generally called? The words "system" and "application" are most often used. Some differentiate; one common pattern is that a "system" contains "applications." Another reading is that the "application" is the software, while the "system" includes the hardware, databases, people, and so forth. (This is a sound representation, but becomes problematic in environments that share servers or databases.)

Others simply equate system (sometimes qualified as "software system") with application, arguing that to attempt a distinction is hopeless. We use the two interchangeably and refer generally to the software world. Systems run on servers and depend on databases.

As noted elsewhere in this book, a defined process must be agreed on to add new applications/systems formally to the portfolio. Otherwise, redundancy and conflicting logical conceptions will result.

8.6.3 Systems and Components

By this approach, a system contains components. That is, the logical concept of system is a grouping of physical executable components. Now, if you sit down at a console in the data center, you don't see a "system." The Quadrex system mentioned earlier might be a collection of components: **qdx.exe, qdclt.dll, qdyr23.dll,** and so forth, demonstrating the key logical/physical nature of the problem. How does a person know that the logical system concept Quadrex is embodied in those cryptic executables?

A mapping is necessary, a cross-reference something like this:

System	Component
Quadrex	qdx.exe
Quadrex	qdclt.dll
Quadrex	qdyr23.dll

A simplified information model might be:

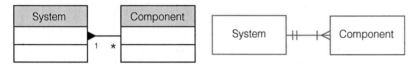

Simple in concept, but challenging in practice. Few IT shops have such a comprehensive cross-referencing, which can lead to problems in areas such as:

- Licensing compliance
- Correct version management
- Understanding the business and technical dependencies on a server

Configuration and asset management are particularly concerned with these issues.

8.6.4 Logical to Physical Traceability

The concept of application or system is a logical concept, an abstraction that allows the IT person to concisely represent a complex reality. As a logical concept, it fits comfortably with enterprise architecture, and the ICC should partner with enterprise architects in defining the application portfolio. This concept of system is crucial in understanding and managing the complexity of systems integration.

We know that systems talk to each other, typically to exchange data. Informally, whiteboard sessions often use the following kind of diagram:

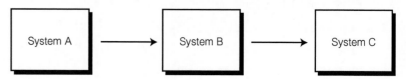

However, these high-level system abstractions obscure considerable detail. The integration problem encompasses a bewildering variety of technologies: messaging, FTP, file sharing, database middleware, RMI, application servers, message brokers, and more.

Consider a subset of the preceding example:

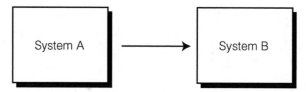

Physically, this diagram might be implemented by the architecture below:

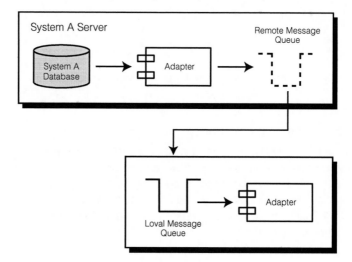

Just as a data management group needs to know the mappings of the logical model to its physical RDBMS instances, an integration group needs to know the mappings of architectural, system-to-system data flows to the physical paths of the data being interchanged. These flows use messaging infrastructures, plain FTP, and other infrastructures. This is where configuration management comes in, which at its most mature provides a complete reference for all the devices and all their software.

However, integration dependencies are a very advanced problem relative to most configuration management tools and practices today. Integration metadata stretches the configuration management envelope. For example, a robust configuration management capability might map intraserver dependencies (executables to their shared libraries). Integration metadata requires mapping cross-server dependencies. For example, a messaging channel typically will affect two servers, so the middleware creates a dependency between those servers. This point brings us to a discussion of managing dependencies.

8.7 Dependency Management: Connections, Connections

8.7.1 Graph Theory: The Foundation

Metadata, or IT configuration management data, presents unique problems compared with the data that IT manages on behalf of its partners. Financial, logistical, and HR data has deep roots in paper-based history. A purchase order or a hiring authorization message can be traced directly back to its roots in the forms once routed by interoffice mail to in-baskets throughout pre-electronic corporations.

When you look at a sales journal, or a stack of purchase orders, you generally see consistency: The data model is the same for all the information.

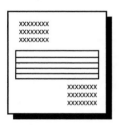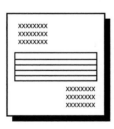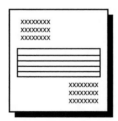

The data also has limited interconnections. A purchase order may reference common employee lookup tables and product tables, resulting in data models that are relatively straightforward to understand:

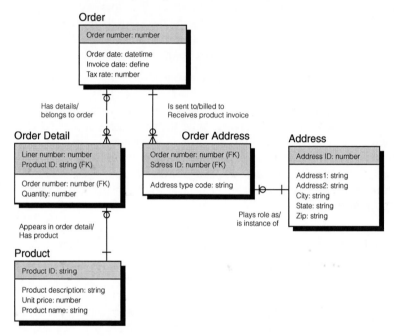

With metadata, everything gets much more complex. Data metadata is the most tractable; tables (or entities) have columns (or attributes), so building simple data dictionaries is straightforward.

But when we move beyond this straightforward data into technical metadata (that is, configuration management), the data starts to take on new characteristics. In mathematical terms, it becomes graph based; that is, it looks like this:

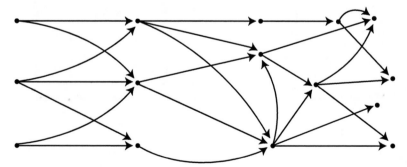

This kind of data presents well-known problems in storage, querying, and presentation because it requires "any to any" data models and can rapidly become complex to the point of incomprehensibility.

This type of data is not typically encountered in business-centric systems that are the successors to forms-based paper processes. It is the kind of data stored by configuration management databases, CASE tools, and metadata repositories when they move into managing software engineering artifacts and technical metadata, such as data models, network topologies, and integration flows.

8.7.2 Connecting Applications

Data dictionaries typically answer well-defined questions, such as:

- What columns are on this table?
- What tables are in this schema?
- What schemas are in this database?

Integration metadata, by contrast, is concerned with end-to-end semantics:

- Given system A and system B, show how data moves between them.

When you say that a system may be connected to any other system, you are calling for a data model that essentially looks like this:

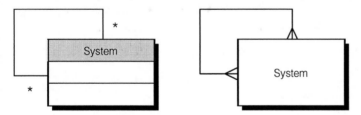

These structures are a standing joke among seasoned data modelers because someone can "solve" any data modeling problem with them in theory. Although we have little choice in using something like them to represent system interlinkages, careless use can be misleading. Consider this example again:

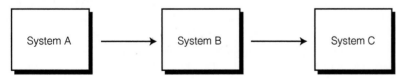

The casual viewer may well assume that the connections between A-B and B-C have something to do with each other. Apparently the diagram shows that the same data is flowing from A to C (it is transitive). But nothing of the sort may be true, which is why large graphs of systems can be so misleading. Systems A and B may be exchanging personnel data, while systems B and C are exchanging financial data, and the two exchanges may have no dependency or relationship to each other at all.

The following information model may help to clarify things:

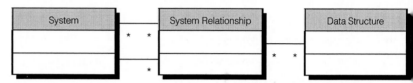

This model gives us much more richness. First, it refiles "system relationship" as a first-class entity, which allows us to associate attributes and other entities. There are many different kinds of relationships, which may, for example, be implemented in turn by infrastructure and supported by parties.

The preceding model allows us to capture the precise data semantics flowing across the integration, and it would be suitable, for example, for a message queuing architecture. When the relationship is tied to a data structure, it becomes possible to constrain a complex graph to interesting subsets of systems that are exchanging the same data topic.

Logically, such a query would read something like this:

> **Find all systems**
>
> **joined by relationships**
>
> **where the relationships are tied to data structure A.**

(Note that relationships involving data structures are only one kind of relationship; the system relationship entity would be a subtype in a more robust model.)

Such queries are an order of magnitude more difficult than the data questions listed at the beginning of this section. In the data world, we know that schemas contain tables, which contain columns. With integration flows, we have no such certainty. Generally, we can know neither the number of "hops," nor their type, between two endpoints. Finally, because it is a graph, the best way to portray it is graphically, and this presents another set of issues in human comprehension if it is too complex.

A brief discussion of another means of isolating meaningful dependency subsets using the concept of business process follows.

8.7.3 Logical/Physical in a Graph World

The logical/physical problem is especially acute with integration, because both the logical and physical integration worlds require graph structures to handle (they are both hairballs), and traceability is a major issue. That is, unlike the data domain, where we can trace a logical entity relationship diagram ERD relatively easily to its physical implementations (given a well-managed data administration capability), tracing high-level information flows to their physical implementations is a significantly harder challenge. Physical hardware, software components, and virtual constructs must all be supported. The problem is not just one hairball, but at least two, and each and every strand of hair in one ball must be tied to its counterpart(s) in another.

Appendix A

About Informatica

Informatica Corporation is a leading provider of enterprise data integration software. Using Informatica products, companies can access, integrate, migrate, and consolidate enterprise data across systems, processes, and people to reduce complexity, ensure consistency, and empower the business. More than 2,100 companies worldwide rely on Informatica for their end-to-end enterprise data integration needs. For more information, please visit www.informatica.com.

Informatica products are designed to help our customers simplify their IT infrastructure by providing a single platform for all enterprise data integration initiatives. Informatica products empower the business user with holistic information, reduce the cost and complexity of enterprise IT infrastructure for the IT manager, and provide increased productivity to IT practitioners, which improves their responsiveness to the business. These capabilities are delivered through a service oriented architecture to enable the IT architect to maximize existing and future flexibility.

Appendix A

Appendix B

About Integration Consortium

Integration Consortium is a nonprofit, leading industry body responsible for influencing the direction of the integration industry. Its members champion integration acumen by influencing standards, establishing guidelines and best practices, sponsoring research, and articulating strategic and measurable business benefits. The Integration Consortium's motto is "Forging Integration Value."

The Integration Consortium was formed in July 2001 after a number of Integration industry leaders identified, as a business priority, the requirement to ensure that industry trends were communicated with reliability and dependability. The integration industry is rapidly evolving and, as a result, a need to promote a greater understanding of, and establish guidelines for, integration business practices was identified.

The mission of the member-driven Integration Consortium is to strive for universal seamless integration in a way that engages industry stakeholders from the business, technology, and academic communities.

Among the sectors represented by the Integration Consortium membership are end-user corporations, independent software vendors (ISVs), hardware vendors, systems integrators, academic institutions, nonprofit institutions, and individual members, as well as various industry leaders. Information on the Integration Consortium is available at www.integrationconsortium.org.

This book, *Integration Competency Center*, is a wonderful demonstration of the insightful thought leadership demonstrated by our contributing members, John Schmidt of World Wide Integration, Inc. and David Lyle of Informatica. The Integration Consortium is honored to sponsor this dynamic book, which sheds some light and clarity on one of the most fundamental components of the enterprise integration holistic solution. *Integration Competency Center* is the cornerstone for any organization that is building a sustainable business integration strategy. This book should be a new industry point of reference on the topic.

The members of the Integration Consortium continually find new and innovative ways for key industry stakeholders to work together in an environment that gives all participants the opportunity to communicate and together achieve best-of-breed solutions. The *Integration Competency Center* publication is a shining example of collaboration at its finest.

Michael Kuhbock, Chairman & Founder
Integration Consortium

Appendix C

References

A vast array of information is available on various aspects of integration. Here are some of the most useful ones for any organization with an interest in establishing an integration competency center.

IC	The Integration Consortium (IC) provides a wide variety of white papers, user groups, and other resources to support efforts to develop an ICC. The IC was formed after a number of integration industry leaders identified as a priority the need to ensure that industry trends were communicated reliably and dependably (www.integrationconsortium.org).
TBI	Total business integration (TBI) is a methodology initially developed at Johnson & Johnson and currently available through the IC. This methodology is considered a full life-cycle integration methodology with the goal of providing transparency of the solution from the requirements phase through delivery, ongoing operations, and ultimately retirement. TBI includes a set of tools that project teams can use "out of the box" to create integration deliverables without having to create their own templates and processes (http://www.integrationconsortium.org/page.php?content=TBI_TOC).
SEI	The Software Engineering Institute (SEI) is a federally funded research and development center sponsored by the U.S. Department of Defense through the Office of the Under Secretary of Defense for Acquisition, Technology, and Logistics. The SEI's core purpose is to help others make measured improvements in their software engineering capabilities (www.sei.cmu.edu).

CMM	The SEI's Capability Maturity Models (CMMs) assist organizations in maturing their people, process, and technology assets to improve long-term business performance. The SEI has developed CMMs for software, people, and software acquisition and assisted in the development of CMMs for systems engineering and integrated product development (http://www.sei.cmu.edu/cmm/).
PMI	The Project Management Institute (PMI) provides global leadership in the development of standards for the practice of the project management profession throughout the world. PMI's premier standards document, *A Guide to the Project Management Body of Knowledge* (PMBOK® Guide), is a globally recognized standard for managing projects in today's marketplace. The PMBOK Guide is approved as an American National Standard by the American National Standards Institute (ANSI). PMI is committed to the continuous improvement and expansion of the PMBOK Guide, as well as the development of additional standards (www.pmi.org).
PMBOK	As defined in the 2000 edition of *A Guide to the Project Management Body of Knowledge* (PMBOK Guide), project management is the application of knowledge, skills, tools, and techniques to a broad range of activities to meet the requirements of a particular project. Project management consists of five processes—initiating, planning, executing, controlling, and closing—as well as nine knowledge areas. These nine areas center on management expertise in a project's Integration, scope, time, cost, quality, human resources, communications, risk management, and procurement (http://www.pmi.org/info/pp_pmbok2000welcome.asp).
OGC	The Office of Government Commerce (OGC) is an independent Office of the U.K. Treasury reporting to the Chief Secretary. It is responsible for a wide-ranging program that focuses on improving the efficiency and effectiveness of central civil government procurement, and it has an important role in developing and promoting private sector involvement across the public sector. The OGC owns the ITIL copyright (http://www.ogc.gov.uk/).

ITIL	IT Infrastructure Library (ITIL) is the most widely accepted approach to IT service management in the world. ITIL provides a cohesive set of best practices, drawn from the public and private sectors internationally. It is supported by a comprehensive qualification scheme, accredited training organizations, and implementation and assessment tools. The best-practices processes promoted in ITIL both support and are supported by the British Standards Institution's Standard for IT Service Management (BS15000) (http://www.ogc.gov.uk/index.asp?id=2261).
ITscout	ITscout (http://www.itscout.com) is a Website that organizes, classifies, and categorizes a broad range of IT information related to technologies. It uses visual taxonomies to help find a particular vendor and includes hyperlinks to product pages and vendor Websites. It also provides a ranking of products based on the views of visitors to the site (www.flashmapsystems.com).
OMG	The Object Management Group (OMG) is an open membership, not-for-profit consortium that produces and maintains computer industry specifications for interoperable enterprise applications. Its flagship specification is the model-driven architecture (MDA) based on the modeling specifications MOF, UML, XMI, and CWM (http://www.omg.com/).
MDA	Model-driven architecture (MDA) is a comprehensive approach to information systems engineering that systematically addresses the complete life cycle of automating business processes through software. MDA focuses on formalizing and standardizing the artifacts associated with designing, deploying, integrating, and evolving supporting software applications (http://www.omg.org/mda/).
TOGAF	The Open Group Architecture Framework (TOGAF) is an architecture development methodology that any organization can use freely to develop an information systems architecture for use within that organization. TOGAF has been developed and continuously evolved since the mid-'90s by the Open Group and its members (http://www.opengroup.org).

ERP4IT	www.erp4it.com is a Weblog dedicated to the subject of enterprise IT automation, or "enterprise resource planning for IT" (www.bijonline.com/Article.asp?ArticleID=799). This is not the automation of business process by IT; rather, it is IT automating itself. This site provides some insightful thought leadership for anyone concerned with enterprise architecture, metadata, application portfolio management, or IT service management.
Web services	A Web service is a software construct that exposes business functionality using Internet-related technologies. The core standards are SOAP, WSDL, HTTP, and UDDI. Many IT groups use these standards for internal request/reply interfaces between applications and do not actually expose the interfaces to the Internet. For a more complete definition, visit the Web Services Interoperability Organization Website at www.ws-i.org.
itSMF	The IT Service Management Forum (itSMF) is an internationally recognized independent organization dedicated to IT service management. It is a not-for-profit organization, wholly owned and principally operated by its membership. The itSMF is a major influence on, and contributor to, industry "best practices" and standards worldwide, working in partnership with a wide range of governmental and standards bodies (http://www.itsmf.com/).

About the Authors

John Schmidt

John Schmidt is President of the Integration Consortium, a nonprofit organization promoting integration best practices. Mr. Schmidt has practiced as an information systems professional for 28 years and has experience in a wide range of industries, including retail, communications, and banking, as well as education and government. He has a record of consistent leadership in breaking new ground and driving business results.

Mr. Schmidt is a frequent speaker on the topic of integration and has written a number of articles on the subject. He can be contacted by email at john.schmidt@integrationconsortium.com.

David Lyle

David Lyle is the vice president of product strategy at Informatica, where he leads Informatica's research on model-driven architecture as it extends to integration automation. During the early to mid-'90s, Mr. Lyle worked as a data warehousing consultant on several large-scale, massively parallel warehouse projects. From this experience, Mr. Lyle helped found and grow Influence Software from 1996 to 1999 as a pioneering company in the development of analytic applications. Informatica bought Influence at the end of 1999 and since then, Mr. Lyle has helped expand Informatica's data integration platform and metadata technologies, creating several patent-pending technologies for the company.